BEGGARS IN VELVET

BEGGARS IN VELVET

Carlyle Marney

ABINGDON PRESS

New York   Nashville

CONTENTS

III. THE HOPE WE HAVE

Hark, hark, the dogs do bark,
    The beggars are coming to town,
Some in rags,
    Some in tags,
        And some in velvet gowns.

I

THE LIFE WE LEAD

THE BUSY MAN

SOME OLD PICTURES THE CHILDREN FOUND REMINDED ME OF A NEIGHBOR I knew in a choice little town. He owned the waterworks, an automobile agency, a public garage, and at least one side of the downtown business section. From the waterworks he got an ulcer; from the auto agency he got high-blood pressure; out of his garage he got a bad case of the hives; and I suppose it was the real estate that gave him the "fidgets" he had when he was about forty-five years old. His condition was further complicated by his hobby; he read all the books he could find about all the things that could be wrong with the human body. Somewhere in the course of each book he would contract every disease that he read about. He "suffered" every weakness he could inherit, and every virus he could pick up. Eventually he began to read psychology manuals, and he caught all the mental troubles described in each book. Finally somebody said, "Well, Roy, if you are that sick maybe you ought to just pack up and go off up north to one of those big clinics and let them work you over."

I noticed that my neighbor was gone ten days or so, then I ran into him at the post office on the day he got back. He had a glazed, dazed look on his face. I said, "Now that you are a graduate of that famous clinic what did you find out about yourself?"

He said, "Well, I found out a lot, but they gave me—well, it is just the toughest prescription I ever heard of."

I asked, "Can they do you any good?"

"Oh," he said, "they said they could cure me but it is going to be mighty expensive."

"Well, what is it going to cost?"

"They said the only way I could get well would be to sell the waterworks, and my automobile agency, and my garage, and all my real estate except one house; move into the house and adopt eleven kids, get me a job on a railroad section, live on beans, cabbage, and hard bread, and you know I can't do that." He didn't, but the doctor who prescribed for my friend was more than half serious.

Let me show you another kind of busy man. Mr. Tom is a stone mason. For weeks he has been chipping out rock and mixing his own mortar, laying walls, cornices, and supports for some new buildings at our youth camp. You never know in my business when you are going to need some other means of income so I have been laying stone during the camp season, learning from Mr. Tom. For example, I learned one thing—you are not supposed to "plaster" rocks, you are supposed to "joint" them—"don't plaster those rocks, son, just joint them."

I wish you knew Mr. Tom. He is a big man with heavy arms and huge shoulders. I would say he is more than seventy and a widower now. Somehow, in two weeks of casual, then deeper, association with this fine craftsman, I got the notion that he is one of the few men I have met who has just about all a man needs. I don't know whether he knows that he is a tremendously wealthy man or not; but I discovered in my hours of working with him that there are a few things a man can get with which he can go a long way.

The first thing I caught from Mr. Tom is that a man who is going to live in this crazy world of ours needs some solitude. Not many of us can take a job at half price and stay three months just for solitude's sake. But Tom does. He goes for days without seeing another human being, he sits on the side of a hill and cuts a rock to size, he puts it in on a bed of mortar, and seals it; then he stops, gets a drink of water, looks across the lake to the hills where he was born seventy years ago, and rests, and thinks. He works, and rests, and thinks. Not many of us are stone masons. But any man in the most crowded kind of office, in the busiest kind of department store, even a bus driver, needs some solitude; he needs some time when his soul comes back to him; when he comes alive; when he asks himself some questions.

I have observed a second thing in watching Tom live these weeks. A man needs to do some creative manual work. Leo Tolstoy wrote about this, but Tolstoy was a man of great wealth; he owned tens of thousands of acres of wheat land; he had two or three thousand peasants working his land for him; he could afford to *enjoy* creative manual work. Tolstoy put down that any man who makes his living sitting down needs to do four hours a day of manual work. Tolstoy could afford to quit whatever he was doing and go saw wood any four hours that he wished. Perhaps his advice is not very practical. But I know that in the life I live nothing has quite the same kind of healing as creative manual work.

In order to live well, and to live with some kind of ease in this fear-ridden world a man needs a code. He needs a set of values to go by. He needs some sort of way of measuring the various facets, lines, cornices, corners, grades, and levels of his life. I expect a man who has spent fifty or sixty years as a stone mason has a pretty good idea of what is square and what is true, what can be used, what can be rejected. I am sure he has discovered over and again the truth of the saying that the stone that was rejected has become the head of the corner. More than once I have seen Tom throw away a rock that was ugly or misshapen, and then I have seen him go back late in the afternoon when he needed just one rock to finish up a wall, and according to the code he had for his work, pick up the rock he had rejected.

And a man needs something else; deep within himself he needs a living loyalty and devotion. Tom speaks frequently of his great love for his children and his grandchildren. They come out to visit him sometimes where he lives on the job in his nice trailer house, and I treasured the loyalty and love that he had for his children. But I found in him also a higher type of devotion. I happened by his trailer in midafternoon. He had stopped late for lunch, had first taken a nap. When he awakened he had broiled a piece of meat out of his own locker and with a great chunk of bread was enjoying his lunch when I dropped in for a visit. I noticed a book open on the table and casually, perhaps too curiously, glanced over his shoulder; he was reading the New Testament. Apparently it was a habit of his to build himself little altars through the day; not out of rock, not out of mortar, but out of high thoughts from the kind of book he reads. Man is too busy when he gets away from these four basic needs of the spiritual man: solitude, work, a code to live by, and a center for his loyalties.

With another friend, I stepped into a Washington cab at the entrance to the Mayfair. "Where to?" the cabbie asked. And my friend replied, "It doesn't matter, cabbie, I've got business everywhere!" He is sick, too, and wishes he could lay rocks into a wall, and watch his work, and rest.

STIR - CRAZY

Some visitors had come to see all that was going on at Mar-bridge Ranch. They had been taken to see the ceramic section, laundry, work shed, farm fields, the turkey houses, the pigpens, and came at last to several cages of white Leghorn fryers that were being raised for ranch use. Here the chickens never touch the ground; they get all the water they want, they have all the feed they can eat, and they are supposed to stand there day and night and drink water and eat good rich chicken feed until they are ready to be eaten.

One of our visitors noticed that these chickens had a strange look in their eyes; some of them had their neck feathers pulled off, some had their heads through little holes in the cage, some had been pecked. He said to one of the boys guiding him through, "Do you suppose these chickens in this cage are happy?" His young escort said, "Of course not, they are stir-crazy! All of them!"

Are you stir-crazy? At the zoo the children used to say that the lions and the leopards and the hyenas particularly seemed to be mad. They paced back and forth nervously, aimlessly, with a fierce eagerness to be rid of the bars that shut them in. They seemed insane. All of them. People get this way too! The difference between us, the animals in the zoo, and the chickens in the pens, is that we build our own pens. We build them all our lives, even before adulthood, and we build them out of such flimsy material. I saw a man at a rodeo leading a stallion by a thread. We can be held by such tiny little strings. A lady who works downtown, does her work at home, does her work at church, at the clubs, and who belongs to a half a dozen other organizations, sooner or later gets stir-crazy. "Do you reckon she is happy?" No. She is stir-crazy.

You notice this in adolescence, too. Some of the fourteen-year-olds that I know belong to a band, a choir, a Sunday-school class, a

15

young-people's group, a Y-Teen group, Girl Scouts, take several courses in school, belong to a neighborhood gang, and are supposed to be in between times, a daughter. These kids are not just adolescent, they are stir-crazy too!

But this is not just a modern problem. It was a problem in the life of Augustine who cried, "Then I collected myself from the dispersion to which I had given myself, then I recalled myself from the many to the one."

Look at the various kinds of pens that we build for ourselves. People who live on a stated income frequently build a pen out of obligations they have incurred for things they want in advance of their ability to pay. They become stir-crazy because there is no room to move around at all; any family emergency throws them into a major seizure of some sort. Again, people can build a set of pens for themselves out of the ideas they are willing to let live in their lives. They become a people committed to a way of life, religiously, philosophically, or culturally, so narrow and tight and squeezing that they wind up as rigid little groups with rigid little patterns of rigid little ideas and they never know that the world is bigger than the backyard of ideas which they have made into a cage. I have friends who have built pens for themselves out of their own appetites, their own indulgences, and their own way of life. This leaves no time or space for participation in new things, fresh things, real things. They are already committed to such a narrow pathway that life has become this and this—and no more. This is a stircraze that comes on a man who limits himself to too small a way of life.

Men, also, may become stir-crazy through their own ambitions. Ambition will focus and with this comes such a reliance upon the fulfillment of ambition that any sort of frustration creates a kind of pen in which their necks are caught like people used to be pilloried in stocks.

The head of one of the largest businesses of the nation died three or four years ago in an Eastern city. Because I had known him in earlier years, a friend sent me a news clipping and it required two newspaper columns to list the organizations to which the man was related. Though he was one of this country's great men, in some ways, I would never have called him a free man, for he belonged to everybody!

We get so involved in so many obligations and ideas and appetites and ambitions and organizations and drives and habits that freedom becomes to us simply a word somebody else uses. Now certainly no one of us is going to be entirely free. Certainly, as with all governments, universities, churches, we are proprietary institutions; that is to say, we are owned by something. But a man can be freer than he is, and he doesn't have to be stir-crazy. This, I say, is primarily true because his slavery and his pens are his own. I am not willing at all to claim that we are placed in these slaveries without any choice, or desire, or control. I am not at all willing to believe that life is such a determinism as this. I am claiming that we make our own slavery, we build our own pens, we create our own crazes. It is up to a man to identify his slaveries. Once he sees that to which he is enslaved, then he must decide whether or not it is worth his life, whether or not it is worth his devotion. If it is, he keeps it; if it isn't he finds some other way to deal with it.

Are you stir-crazy? My friend looked at the crate of white Leghorn chickens and said, "Are they happy?" Well, happiness is no better a goal for men than chickens, but "stir-craziness" keeps us from more worthy goals. It denies us the power to focus on the one center of life that is most worthwhile. Whatever that center is ought to have our highest devotion.

CONTRIVED DISTRACTIONS

Do you live the life of "contrived distractions"? A minister knocked on a door out in Tarrytown this afternoon and an eight-year-old boy came to the door. "Son, where is your daddy?"

"Playing golf."

"Where is your mamma?"

"She has gone to the bridge club."

"Well, where is your big brother?"

"Oh, he is over at football practice."

"Is your sister at home?"

"She has a date this afternoon."

"Well, what are you doing at home?"

"Mister, I wouldn't be at home except that I've got the tomcat in the freezer trying to turn him into a polar bear." Now, this boy was living the life of contrived distraction.

Most any time a man sits and gets quiet and thinks, he sees something desperately wrong in the middle of his life. It is here that he contrives some distraction to divert him. The mystery as to what life is all about looms up in front of him, and therefore, he doesn't stop if he can help it. By not stopping, he will not be confronted with the mystery as to what it is that is missing in his life. He joins the race, the mad rush to live the life of contrived distraction: juke boxes, coffee breaks, holidays, novelty merchandise. In his reading habits, TV habits, movie habits, radio habits, not to speak of his petty vices, he manages to keep himself constantly interrupted with a moving chain of events or happenings or occurrences that are deliberately, it seems, contrived to disturb or distract so that he never will really be alone for a moment.

Now this is not just a surface occurrence; it is really one of the deepest character traits of the race and of our time. I believe this life of contrived distraction might be something of a key to Goethe's immortal *Faust*. I think it lies somewhere in the background of Dante Alighieri's *Inferno,* for the object of Dante, I am sure, was not so much an understanding of hell as it was an attempt to escape earth—and reality and the situation.

Now what is this situation from which men desire to escape? At bottom, man is trying to escape the self, where the self is, and as the self is. He cannot bear to be altogether as he is and confined to what he is, as he is; consequently he cannot dare to be really alone without something to distract him. He cannot afford to be as he is, consequently he does not like to be alone unless he has contrived some distraction to keep him from focusing. Let me illustrate.

He does not wish to be alone with the mystery of birth—therefore he isolates himself with a stack of magazines while his son or daughter is being born. He does not wish ever to be absolutely alone with the mystery of life, and therefore he completely covers himself up with one enterprise after another. He does not dare be really alone with the mystery of death, and therefore he camouflages the whole thought, the whole experience, the whole way of looking at the thing with a suburban life, and a "garden of paradise" kind of approach to the reality of the mystery of death. He has his radio on while he is shaving; and strangely enough that moment when he confronts himself in a mirror with a razor in his hand is about the only moment of the day when he has a chance to talk with himself. But he turns the radio on so that he won't interrupt himself while he is shaving. If, of course, he uses an electric razor, then the radio is not very practical and he makes his own music as he goes. I know a preacher who carries a dictaphone in his automobile so that he can always have a real reason for escaping himself. We eat to a jukebox, travel on a timetable, buy on installments, and join a half-dozen mystery religions; we are besieged by callers, waiters, checkers, and telephones, and seldom know what we have missed.

I stopped by for Washington the other day to get him to go shoe a horse of mine; while I was waiting a big bird dog came tearing around the house and fell into a perfect point on a *bumblebee.* Joe Evans had a pack of bear dogs that ran off on a bear hunt, fell to chasing a rabbit, and ended up barking at a hole—these are lives of contrived distraction.

Sometimes in an attempt to escape the life of contrived distractions, a man actually goes to church. And when he gets in church, the situation is really not much better, for there is seldom a place for the confrontation that he needs; the contrived distractions are there too. And if they are not within himself, they are sometimes in the service; they are in the boring list of announcements, or in the printed order of service. There is never any moment of real Holy, Holy, Holy. We usually manage to evade the moment of mystery. Strange, isn't it, how we escape the Holy by being more religious? It is strange, isn't it, how we evade the great Other, by our constant refusal to be us? How we will flee the higher by our attempt to preserve the lower; how, by refusing to be really ourselves, we miss an encounter with Him. Strange, isn't it, how in our pitiable little lives we go on obscuring mystery with the obvious?

A fine teacher of English literature retired last year, and he was desperate when he got away from his literary works until he could make himself agent for a string of rental houses. He had to contrive some distractions to fill him in his solitude.

I know that I am a whole lot better at diagnosis than I am at therapy, but I try to find the moment, make the moment, live the moment when without any interruption (without even being willing to be interrupted) I withdraw from all these contrived distractions and allow myself to confront God. By life, birth, death, its mysteries, its infinite horizons, I find myself frequently in that moment in the presence of the Holy. In this life of contrived distractions, try to find "the moment." It might grow to last a half hour; it might become tremendously important; it might be the opening of a door through which you would come into a life marked by something more than the list of contrived distractions through which we live, and in which we find a sorry reason for existence. Find "the moment" and let it grow as it will.

RIGHT ON TIME

THE AVERAGE MAN LIKES THINGS TO COME OUT RIGHT. HERE IN THE Western world it is a rule, a law of life, that all men like things to come out right. Whether a fellow is building a birdhouse, or putting in plumbing to a bath tub, he likes for the fixtures to fit; he likes for things to come out right.

This began very early at your house, for one of your first toys, almost as soon as you could sit up alone, was likely a set of blocks of some sort. The earliest educational tools are designed to teach children that some things fit and some things do not fit. I suppose all this is very good, for a youngster begins to get a sense of order, a sense of decency, a sense of rightness, a sense of this fitting here and this fitting there. We like for things to come out right. We even take it so far that we like for our payments to come out even. You go all the way through life living with this principle and the last thing that is done for you, the digging of your grave, is done with mathematical regard for precise dimensions.

21

One of the strange things, and yet not so strange, is that the more we love order, and the more we like for things to come out right, the more highly frustrated we are when we are unable to make things fit. Perhaps you have seen a little fellow with his new wooden hammer and set of blocks take the hammer and literally pound and scream in frustration because he couldn't make things come out right. Certainly you know how it is to come home and get along miserably with all the members of the family simply because things would not come out right at your work.

Now we carry this further—we not only want our blocks to fit, our payments to fit, and our coffins to fit, we want life to come out right—right for us. And we are willing to pay a fantastic price to be sure that life comes out as we have previewed it, and prejudged it, and have attempted to prearrange it. We will make most any kind of sacrifice to be sure that a given venture comes just as we wish it to come, and ends on schedule just as we wish it to end. I know men who have gotten so accustomed to this way of living that a vacation for them is really impossible. They carry the precise moment of arrival and departure at every little place they intend to pass. They make a burden and an agony out of all of life's short journeys, assuming, I am sure, that some virtue is gathered by staying on that precise schedule so that when all is totaled at the end of the line, life will have come out right.

Carry this just another step along the line and we see that mostly what we are seeking is some principle to make life make sense. The moment a man starts consciously looking for something to make life make sense, the moment he starts looking for a hook upon which he can hang things, that moment he is really a philosopher. Now he may not be a very good philosopher; he may not be very erudite and he may come up with some very wrong answers, but he is doing the philosopher's task; that is, he is looking for some

22

principle by which things can be made to make sense. We look for this in some set of ideas. Many millions of people take refuge in one institution or another in the hope to make life safe. Some make life hang on beauty. They are artists, in the best sense of the word. Some of us make life hang on the fact and experience of communion, with each other, and with God. These people are people of religion. Some people make knowledge the peg on which they wish to hang all of life. And before they know it they are scientists, for that is the concern of science. Others make life hang on what is good, or what is right, or what is valuable. These may be all the various levels of moralists up to the level where a man becomes vitally and really concerned with ethics. But whether you are artist, or religionist, or scientist, or man of ethics, regardless of what you are, mostly we look for one thing to trust to make life come out just right with no tattered ends, no clutter. Some find it, some do not.

Did you see the television play, "The Hanging Judge"? A judge was convinced beyond a shadow of doubt that given a proper indictment, and a proper following of the established legal procedure in the British courts, that justice would always be done. This particular judge staked his very life on the fact that the law is always right in Great Britain. He had no reservations whatsoever that it could ever have been possible for him to have sentenced an innocent man to hang when a jury of that man's peers had pronounced him guilty. The law in his judgment was perfect—it would make things come out right; and therefore it would have been impossible for the British legal system to make such a gross error as to allow an innocent man to go to his death. In the climax of the play, the judge charged himself with a murder, pays the fabulous price of being willing to confess a crime he did not commit, in order that his god might not die; that his great idea of what would make life come out right in the end would not be sinned against.

It is the everyday experience of all that in spite of our search for some principle, some idea, or some institution that will make life sit up and beg, sooner or later life just will not behave; it won't sit up and beg; it won't follow our rules; it will contradict our idea.

There are those in every town I have ever known, in every church I have ever known, who will take even the gospel of the Lord Christ and attempt to make out of it a legalism—a pat little set of rules that will fit every situation. I know you inflexible fathers with inviolable rules who, by the use of these inviolable rules, manage to be the enemy of your own children. You have a pre-fabricated kind of religion with answers made up in advance; and then, bang! The trouble involves *your* son, or it is *your* daughter, or it is *you,* and you are involved in a situation where your love will not let your flat, pat answers work. Then you start looking for an answer with personal values.

This above everything the Christian gospel has: a concern for personality. And this is why you can't make the things that happen to you and to yours fit into your little grooves. There is no flat gospel answer. Whether you are concerned with adultery, or a minor act of juvenile delinquency, there is no flat gospel answer that says "do this" every time "this" comes up. In the gospel love is involved with the caught one, and all who are caught are persons. This is the meaning of the Cross.

In Ian Maclaren's *Beside the Bonnie Briar Bush* a father learned that he could not bury his daughter because she had done wrong. Though he had scratched her name from the family Bible, she came back and made him love her. And under the name by which he had buried her he had to bring her back to life because he had discovered that love can never find a pat, flat answer. Life just won't come out right, and this is the necessity for forgiveness.

OUTRUNNING OURSELVES

AT MY HOUSE THERE LIVES A TWO-YEAR-OLD IRISH SETTER. HE IS A notorious "character" and quite a would-be traveler. For a while it looked as if someone would steal him at least once a month. He was no good for anything except little girls and when this became clear the thief would throw him out and he would come home after a while. He knows two things—well—three; he knows where the food pan is, he knows the rattle of car keys, and he seems to know the word "go." Anytime a car leaves he expects to be in it, and he sits up in the back seat just like a deacon, as if he were telling you where to go, here and there.

The other day he was half asleep under the dining room table and he heard his mistress say to a neighbor, "Well, I have to go now." And when he heard that word "go" he came roaring out from under the table, turned a corner, hit a freshly waxed floor (swapping ends about four times), slid into every piece of furniture on the back porch twice, turned over three chairs, and broke out through the screen door on the three legs that he had left—all because he heard somebody say "go." He was outrunning himself.

Mankind has learned how to do that now. We are better at it than any Irish setter you ever saw. We can now run so fast, and leave the clock so far behind us, that our stomachs and our nerves and our timer get all out of kilter. In flying to Tokyo we gain some eighteen hours and we travel so much faster than our stomach and nerves and our body can adjust to time changes, that we are a couple of weeks settling down. We wake at two or three o'clock in the morning, ravenously hungry, and are very sleepy about three o'clock in the afternoon. Maybe that is what we are doing everywhere—outrunning ourselves.

An educator said to me, "We need someone to come and try to give us an overview. We can't see it because we are so busy running with details." I find this true in my own life. Once in a while I just have to go hear someone speak or teach who has had time in his own life to keep from getting caught up in the details of everyday living. A safety engineer I heard said that at sixty-five miles an hour people see less than one eighth of what they see at thirty miles an hour, because the side view diminishes in inverse proportion as the speed increases. I am wondering if one of the marks of our times is not that we can be characterized as the people who habitually, everywhere, outrun ourselves. In religious circles we contemplate eternity. And yet some of us have difficulty spending an afternoon alone.

What Makes Sammy Run? was the title of a very interesting book not so long ago. What does make Sammy run? Well, sometimes he gets involved in this business of outrunning himself simply because he doesn't like Sammy and he is trying to get away from him. Sometimes he runs, because he is trying to fill up an empty place. Sometimes he runs just because he is scared, like any young colt will run at some noise. Sometimes he runs just because he doesn't know how to stop. But at any rate it is a tragedy that we are running all the way, and life goes by so fast it blurs. We habitually go through life missing the main thing. We run, I say, like a sophomore driver in a hot rod who can't start up without throwing gravel all over the front yard.

Now what have we outrun in the business of outrunning our-selves—traveling so fast that our bodies and our stomachs and nerves are all out of kilter? What have we outrun in creating all this ulceration of our innards? In one year almost forty thousand people were killed in automobile accidents in the United States. That is slaughter in anybody's language. We are outrunning life.

As vitally important as that question of life itself, we are out-running some other things. For example, we have outrun a really concerned and informed citizenry. I heard an attorney general of one state say that less than 14 per cent of the qualified electoral constituency amended the constitution and elected their officers last year. Again, we have outrun a vital, valid, religious faith; we simply sandwich in our religious lives between runnings here and yon; less than one fifth of the so-called church people of any city have anything to do with any important decision that their church makes. We have outrun the world of literature and music and drama and art. We saturate ourselves with quick doses; we buy little condensations of important new writings in order that in our bridge clubs and other places we can say with that animated expression peculiar to literary discussions: "Oh, yes, I read it last week." We didn't read it last week; we read somebody's hashed up version of it last week. I am saying we have outrun the fundamental verities of our culture. We have outrun true education and—tragedy of tragedies—we have outrun the highest and deepest of personal relations. A man's own family goes by so fast that they become a blur to him. We have outrun personalized Christian service by canning up what we do for our neighbors under the name of great worth-while projects. We have lost the tremendous spiritual impetus of one man doing something for the man who is next to him. And perhaps one of the most tragic things of all, we have outrun the meaning of work and what work ought to be and mean in a man's life. The work that is made by integrity, character, and honest to goodness stick-to-itiveness—the creativeness that ought to come out of a man's personality.

We are paying a high price for driving pretty fast. What are we outrunning? Life itself. Everything important. I can't tell you how to stop. I am not sure I can find out how I can stop; but I am becoming more and more concerned with what I am going to miss if I don't learn how to quit outrunning myself.

THE ULTIMATE CONFUSION

I WAS HAVING COFFEE WITH A FRIEND OF MINE TODAY AND THE WORD "confusion" got into the conversation somehow. Bob said he reckoned that the *ultimate* in confusion would be a termite living in a Yo-yo! A termite in a Yo-yo would live in a limited, provincial world. He would be in a whirling maze, a world that goes nowhere, moves incessantly, and stays on the same string. Most of us live in a tiny round world of our own, whirling at a maddening rate, going nowhere, moving incessantly, sliding always on the same string.

There are two ways people live in this world of confusion, a bad one and a good one. Perhaps I can illustrate it best with the use of a couple of animal stories.

In Buenos Aires the Argentines use great Percheron, Belgian, and Norman draft horses. These are huge animals used to drag unbelievable loads in tremendous wagons. They are always heavily harnessed, heavily loaded, beautifully groomed, bountifully fed, but they have the narrowest set of "blinders" that will fit. Blinders are patches of leather worn alongside the eyes to keep the animals from being diverted by things that are not directly ahead. These huge animals with the blinders pulled tightly over their eyes come to an intersection, hauling this mammoth load behind them with their harness straps taut, bells jingling, trotting in a kind of lock-step. There are no traffic lights, yet these mammoth animals with a load behind them move into eight lanes of traffic without batting an eye—pull right straight out into the street—no pause, no hesitancy, no looking right or left—they just move out into the traffic, majestically. Brakes screech, traffic piles up, people curse, taxi drivers jump out, fenders lock for blocks up the street. There is a particularly powerful Argentine law that prohibits hitting a horse. And so, the wagon drivers just push their teams out into traffic. The horses know there is another world out there; they can hear it well enough, they can smell it well enough, but they have no vision, and somehow they always "know" the traffic will stop to let them across.

Now I have friends who live in life's confused traffic very much like these huge draft horses. They have the notion that somehow in spite of all the confusion the traffic will always stop to let them across. In the meantime, they seem to say, I will do what I can with my own load (and it is always a heavy load if it is my own load). I will not worry about my narrowed vision. I will go on in the middle of this confusion with my blinders pulled right tightly down across my nostrils so that I will never be diverted from the path I am following. I will not worry about any communication with any other being; I will not worry about my lack of awareness—I will not be concerned with what I do not know; I will not accept any responsibility that I haven't got at present. I will simplify my confusion by wearing blinders that keep me from knowing anything else that is going on in anyone's world except my own. I will know nothing except my own; I will commit myself to my own track and no other.

That is one answer for getting through confusion but it is an anti-God, antiman, antisociety, anticulture kind of answer.

On the other hand, there is a better answer. Perhaps it is a little wilder answer, but it certainly is a better answer: At Mount Pleasant, late on an afternoon, I was walking around the town square. It was jammed with traffic from the whole countryside. I was aware, in the noise and confusion, of a particular disturbance down the street. All I could see was the great head and shoulders of a big man wrapped in an army greatcoat sitting high on a wagon seat. As I got closer I could see that it was a high corn wagon being pulled by two very young and very skittish mules. Their ears were forward and they were pulling against each other in the traces; they were dancing all over the street. To my amazement the driver seemed asleep and the reins were slack. All of a sudden the ears on the mules went back to normal and they settled down in the harness and moved on about a half a block. Now a car pulled in front of them again and they just went wild. It was at this point that I became aware of something I had not seen or heard before in the procession—it was the biggest, blackest dog I have ever seen, and he was working about twenty yards ahead of this team of young mules. Any time an automobile got between the dog and the mules, the mules would become frantic, and the dog would literally assault the automobile—he would attack it with roars and showings of teeth. He would dash at the automobile until the driver caught on and pulled out of the lane. As long as the big black dog could be seen by the mules they would work along in quiet harmony, but the moment their point of reference outside themselves was obscured they became frantic again. When the dog was obscured the mules were frantic; when the dog was in place the mules were calm. The difference for them seemed to be a point of reference to measure by; when they lost the point of reference outside themselves the confusions, and smells, and odors and sights of small-town traffic were baffling to them; but when they could see their point of reference they could accept all the confusion, all the disharmony, all the noise and move along in something of peace and calm.

Now this is what true religion is all about. All of us get confused; all of us get caught in disharmony; all of us are involved in the sounds, and noises, and smells of a wide world. Some of us are thrown by them and some of us go round in a circle; others follow a narrowed little path of our own choosing, hoping the traffic will stop; but some of us, though we may be young and skittish, though we may not know very well how to work in harness, we still have a valid point of reference outside ourselves.

I say, this is what religion is all about. It leads men to forsake the narrow paths they would mark out for themselves; it leads men to come out into a world larger than themselves. The true purpose of religion is to furnish a reference point outside myself to which I can look. This establishes communion. This reference point permits orientation. You can tell where you are. That is what Christians mean by their belief in God—the highest reference point we know.

UNEXPECTED HOLIDAY

ALL OVER TOWN I SAW DROVES OF SCHOOL CHILDREN WITH BOREDOM dripping out of their eyes because they were caught in an unexpected holiday. Nothing is more joyously anticipated than a day when unexpectedly school is out—yet nothing is more universally wasted. We are almost always caught flat-footed. The children are underfoot all day and by bedtime mother is completely exhausted. There are no plans made, no reserve of preparation, and certainly on the spur of the moment—no initiative. We just can't think of anything; so the kids wind up at a movie, or sitting on a cold floor in a drugstore leaning back against the counter with the druggist's comic books. What could have been a great day finishes as an utter bore.

Now there are other times in life when we are found almost totally unprepared. Those times when a sudden bad break comes, death, some loss, some great disappointment, or some real de-spair—almost always catch us without reserve of strength and energy.

There are not enough of us like a very gracious friend of mine, now in her eighty-first year, who has told her friends for years and years that they must in good times store up in their minds passages of scripture, things from their own experience, and memories of good days so that when bad times come they will not have to call and ask some friend for help. But not many really take her advice; when a sudden bad break comes, we are almost always unprepared.

On the other hand, we are as frequently unprepared for a good break. We find ourselves here, too, with time on our hands. I know as little about this subject as anyone, and yet even in the kind of life I have been living there comes an hour, or two hours, or half a day—and once in a while there is even a whole day—when all of a sudden I have some time on my hands to use as I will. Yet I am caught almost totally unprepared for the good break. We go on living our lives as if there would never be a change of schedule, as if we would always ride the same bus each day to the same job, as if we would never be required to demonstrate our capacity to change our pace, or to shift gear. We live as though we would live forever at the same rate on the same daily routine, facing the same problems.

I have a good friend who has been a produce man for many years. He habitually gets up at four or half past four, does his early morning work and then has his breakfast along between half-past six and seven o'clock. Nearly every Sunday morning I have breakfast with him on my way to early church. I asked him one morning why he couldn't change pace. "Oh," he said, "for so many years I have gotten up six mornings a week at four or half-past four that

I have never in all those years been able to sleep on the seventh morning." I suppose this way of life is common to us. A good break finds us as unprepared as the bad. And because the good break finds us unprepared, we usually miss it.

This is a backdoor way of approaching the *tension* in which we live. For too many of us any sudden demand for a change of pace is terrifying. I suspect that this is why many men almost suddenly die when they retire from a long life of active service.

The renowned Quaker, Douglas Steere, has a lecture on "The Collected Man and the Uncollected Man." He claims a capitalist is not necessarily a man who has money, but a capitalist is a man *who has no time!* Everything is scheduled for such a man; his breaks are scheduled; his trips are clocked; his life is calendared to death; even his charities are sanitary charities—that is, they are discreet charities enjoyed from a distance and vicariously. It takes such a man the first three weeks of his heart attack to learn how to stay in bed! Sometimes I find him with just the back of his head and one heel touching the bed. This is true because most of us live our lives with no room for the unexpected.

But life really is full of unexpected breaks. You catch a few minutes waiting at the dentist's office; or you have an appointment with someone and he is delayed or he cancels it; or any one of a hundred places in your everyday journey there comes a moment when you have a sudden and unexpected break. It is said of John Wesley, and he reports it himself in his journals, that he read hundreds of books on horseback. Certainly many of his sermons were composed on horseback. He was simply using the breaks that came.

Five charming, brand new teenagers came pell-mell into the drugstore this afternoon and they wore masks of complete boredom. I stopped one whom I knew and asked, "Mary, why are you so bored?" Her eyes fired up and her expression quickened instantly as she denied all possibility of being bored. "Oh, no! How do you like my new hairdo—I have spent half a day on it." Well, the hairdo was worth half a day, but I was really more amused by her next rejoinder to my query when she said, "What did you expect me to do, read the Bible all day?"

There is a possibility of so backlogging our minds with plans of things that we have never gotten to do that when the next good break comes, whether it is ten minutes or a whole week end, there will already be at the tips of your fingers things that you have long desired, expected, and wanted to do, or to be, or to go, or to see; they will be there, and the chance to do them will be there, and your time will all be ready for you. Don't lose these unexpected holidays; they sometimes hold life's choicest moments.

THE ABANDONED BEST

At last after centuries of scientific experiment comes the last word: a truly scientific study about which kind of life is the happiest and the best. Amazingly enough, distinguished social scientists have come out with a claim that the happiest and best life on earth is the life of the peasant in a village. Village life, they say, is life at its very best. Which is, I suppose, to say that the best water comes out of the old oaken bucket; the best kind of garden is the kind that you work out with hand tools; the best bread is baked in a wood-fired oven out of wheat that is cradled by hand, and so on and so on.

There is something about this that is "old hat." There is something about this that is "country" and "gauche." This is a sort of "golden age in the past" business. This is reliance on legend and dream and myth, for not many remind us that there were all kinds of wiggle-tails in the water that was in the old oaken bucket.

For a scientist to say now that families and churches and schools and institutions are at their best among peasants is a shocking sort of thing. It sounds like old man Benjamin Franklin; or it might even go back to the economy of explanation theory—what is simplest is truest. It sounds like *McGuffey's Reader,* or old copy-book stuff. We are reminded of Horatio Alger, the *Rover Boys,* or *Tom Brown's School Days.* We think, too, of those old mottoes and maxims that were nailed around on walls: "Home is where the heart is," and so on.

Peasant life is hard work. It makes a man's thumbs thick enough to cover a half dollar. If it is true that peasant life is best and happiest, it is also true that this life is hardest and shortest.

If it is old hat, if it is out of date, if it is old-fashioned, why do we in this modern age deny that peasant life is best, and yet look all the time for it to come back? Why do we seek its return? For example, we deny the scientific claim that peasant life in a peasant village is best—we deny this by clustering up in hulking big cities of concrete. You can see the denial of the peasant culture in hundreds of cities simply by standing on a hotel deck and counting the square miles of apartment houses. And why, if this peasant life is truly best, do we start the exodus of the best we can rear off to distant places of employment or education? There is a wholesale forsaking of the home village as early as it becomes practicable. Why, if the peasant life is best, do we stay on the move most of our lives? And why is it true that the average American family will make five moves during the time the children are being reared? If it is true that village life is best, why do we go on seeking green pastures for ourselves in far-distant places through more than three fourths of a normal lifetime?

Every visit home that we make we keep assuring those who stay behind how much better village life is. "Oh, John, you just don't know how hot it is, or how rushed we are, how busy we are, how frantic life is in the city," we say. And "you were so smart to stay behind in this village and work in this general store all your life; you just don't know how much better friends are, how much nicer church is, how much closer association you have. . . ." "Oh," you say, "we admit that everybody knows everything about everybody, but this has its advantages and really you were smart to stay behind. Village life is best."

Of course we think village life is best. Why else do some women pay thirty to forty-five dollars for "peasant" blouses, skirts, and so on? And why this strange popularity of "Provincial" or "Early American" furniture? If we do not think the simple uncluttered village life is best, why the strange desire for simplicity in art, artifacts, decor, trim, buildings, and furniture? Even the attraction of trailer life these days is not mobility; the great attraction of living in a trailer is the village life that results when you park. This is apparent or else more trailer dwellers would live off by themselves alone, but they like all the rest of us like to clutter up in some sort of community relationship.

Whether it is true or false that peasant life is best, I am not equipped to say. But there are three or four things that ought to be obvious to us here. Maybe, just maybe, man is better off not to move so much. More people have run off from their native habitat, more people have evaded the responsibility of the provincial area in which they grew up than have found the true green pastures they expected to find by running away. Maybe a fellow is better off not to move so fast, or so much. Maybe, just maybe, things are better where he is than he thinks they are, and just maybe, they really are better where he is than any place he will be able to go.

Even pastors should stay *if* and *when* they can. Pastors need to stay because their congregations are going to move, and if both move no change is possible. I met a couple in a neighboring town recently who had had the same pastor four times in different towns. It would have been simpler if one of them had stayed put.

Most of us are seeking not what we can find but what we have left. Sometimes this search is hopeless. At certain ages we try to go back, and one seldom can. Along about the time a man turns thirty he first seeks to go back. This is where that fabulous play *The Seven Year Itch* came from. About the time a man is forty or forty-five he wishes to go back into young manhood; somewhere between fifty-five and sixty-five, most men try to go back into what they feel they have left behind them, and they get caught in a kind of futility. Meanwhile, the present that I have known many men to abandon was the only thing really worth having.

There is an alternative to this sort of futility. It is making a proper evaluation of the life you are now living, as you now live it, where you now live it. If you will look very carefully you will probably discover that in all your life you never had it so good. Maybe village life is best and maybe most of us still live in villages. More of us, I say, ought to stay put. More of us ought to find life where it is as truly rich, as truly full, as it is meant to be. Increased mobility is seldom the way to find it. I don't know whether village life is best, but I like it where I am.

A TWO-CENT DEAL

I HEARD A CONVERSATION ABOUT FIVE MILLION DOLLARS AND I DIDN'T understand it. I heard another fellow say something about a million-dollar transaction that had just been completed and I can't understand that either. But a two-cent deal I can understand very well.

I saw my youngest walking along toward home with two of her special buddies and stopped to give them a ride. Each was carrying a tall bottle of frosty root beer. They got in the car still pulling on their refreshment, and I said, "Where did you gals pick these up?"

"Oh," they said, "at the filling station across the street." And I said, "What about your deposit? What are you doing with these bottles? Did you just walk off with them?"

"Oh, no, we've got a deal with the filling-station man. We buy a frosty root beer every day after school if we want it, and we pay him just a nickel. We don't have to pay any deposit because in five days that would tie up a dime, and that is just about all we could afford to tie up; in fact this would break us up some weeks," they said. "So he agreed not to charge us a deposit provided we return the bottle on our way to school the next morning. We don't tie up a dime for five days, and he gets his bottle back."

I doubt if it meant anything at all to the filling-station operator, whose name I don't even know; but it suddenly came over me that this fellow who is "making a deal" most days of the week with my little girl and her friends, is helping me rear my daughter. That is to say, in a transaction that involves about 10 per cent of her income he is teaching her that integrity, regularity, and faithfulness to the terms of a bargain are part of any of life's major deals. And he is teaching it with a two-cent bottle. He is helping me rear my daughter by teaching her that there are elements of responsibility with which she must live. Later I noticed two or three little girls in our neighborhood on their way to school, dropping by to make their delivery of the two-cent bottle so that the deal would still be in force for the afternoon.

It is time I remembered the people who are helping me rear my children: the pediatrician, the dentist, the teachers, the mailman, and all those patient neighbors. By the time your children are grown, you have been helped by thousands. True, not all of these transactions in which somebody helps you rear your child involve a deposit; not all of them involve an expenditure of money; not all of them are designed primarily to teach trust, confidence, fidelity, and integrity, but why not make up your own list of all those in town and out of it to whom you are indebted for having helped in some way in the rearing of your children?

There are other children in my neighborhood, children of neighbors, to whom I find myself being grateful because they are the kind of kids they are. Rough, loud, friendly, courteous, grand youngsters; I must be grateful to them. I think of that long list of my own personal friends who have treated my children as if they were persons; and who, every time they treat my children as a person, are helping me rear my child.

Then I think of the scout masters who have given their weeks, evenings, and summers to help daddies be daddies. And I remember that something of fatherhood is involved anywhere and anytime somebody loves a child. This really is what fatherhood means. For the father is one who truly loves. All those who treat your children as persons, all those who give themselves in any teaching relationship: principals of schools, counselors, coaches, pastors, boy friends, girl friends, business people, filling-station operators, and if you press your list on down you will have to include even the pets that belong in the neighborhood—all have helped.

Now, how can I pay this back? Actually, the only way I can

discharge any obligation that I have incurred through the acceptance of the help of those who have helped me rear my children is by my own assumption of the responsibilities for helping everyone I pass. How can I help, except by being in the truest sense of the word a friend to every child I know, and a helper to every parent I pass.

And, really, we've no idea how much even the most casual expression of interest contributes. So I salute a filling-station opperator who with a two-cent deal is helping me teach that she can make transactions if she will hold up her end of the bargain.

There are two-cent deals and there are twenty-dollar deals, but the principle is the same. You see there is enough of this sort of affection and encouragement and inspiration and help around— there is enough to go around, there is enough to spill over every child if we are only aware of the obligations and opportunities that are ours. There is enough leather to cover every foot in the city, still in the stores. There is enough leather, there are plenty of tacks; there are enough shoestrings—it is not leather that is a problem—the problem is whether or not there is enough love to go around, enough help to go around, enough assumption of the responsibility to seeing that there aren't any feet without leather on them. There must be enough love to be sure there are no homes without food in them; enough concern, and love, and interest to be sure there aren't any empty lives that haven't got some affection around them somewhere. I am grateful that a two-cent deal can go on all year, and that this helpful relationship continues throughout the child's girlhood. It will be an inspiration remembered as a thing that happened once, when some grown person acted as if she were a person, and it will spill over into adult life too.

THE THRILLS AROUND YOU

I HAVE BEEN THINKING ALL DAY ABOUT TWO TALL, STRINGY, VERY tired thirteen-year-old boys I met this morning on Tenth Street. "Mister, who lives in that great big white house up there?" "The Governor lives there." Such an expression of awe I think I never saw on human faces. I stopped, leaned against a tree, and watched. To be actually standing in the middle of the state capital looking right there through that fence at the home of the Governor, this literally filled them with awe—such an expression! I have been wishing all day that I could keep whatever it was those youngsters were feeling.

Many things have high value, but they become so common in our lives: flags, institutions, public buildings, all kinds of art, music, drama. How tragic it is when nothing you encounter in your ordinary day's living can put the real light of awe back in your eyes. How sad it is to get old so swifty, and that in our getting old we become so accustomed to the values that are all around us. Not many times in your adult lifetime will you be filled with the awe and wonder these boys were feeling this morning.

Sometimes, almost inadvertently, in some human relation a man stumbles just for the moment into the presence of truth. Truth can come up all around you like a covey of quail into which you have walked; it will flutter its wings and pound and fly away. The same way with beauty—you can see it in such unexpected places—in a little child's eyes, in the way an old man treats his companion, in out of the way places—and just for the moment. How sorry a life we have if we lose our ability to react to the beauty that is around us, or the love, or the pity, or that quality of human life that is most lacking of all—mercy. Sometimes, just for a moment, in the way on old porter will help an old passenger on the train, or in

41

the way some youngster will take particular pains with a little brother or a little sister, or even in the relationships of adults—you will see pictured just for a moment the quality of mercy. How poverty ridden is the life of a man who cannot react to those flags of truth and beauty and those institutions of love and pity and mercy that come up around us. How tragic if they do not move in on us.

To live well in our time requires something much more important than money. To live worthily in our time requires something much more important than patterns, or ideas. To live well and worthily there must always be things that can stir a man. I look in vain for any kind of greatness in a blasé cynicism. There is no depth in bored indifference. There is no continuing virtue for a community in unaroused appreciation. I confess I was moved deeply by the first page of General de Gaulle's memoirs, *The Call to Honour*. This is classic writing; this is beautiful writing, and in the very first paragraph comes this thing that I am talking about. General de Gaulle is speaking,

All my life I have thought of France in a certain way. This is aspired by sentiment as much as by reason. The emotional side of me tends to imagine France like a princess in the fairy stories; or like the Madonna in the frescoes, as dedicated to an exalted and exceptional destiny. Instinctively I have the feeling that providence has created her for complete success or for exemplary misfortunes. If in spite of this, mediocrity should show in the acts of France and her deeds, it always strikes me as an absurd anomaly and must be imputed to the faults of Frenchmen not to the genius of my land.[1]

[1] General Charles de Gaulle, *The Call to Honour* (New York: Simon and Schuster, 1955), p. 1. Used by permission.

What, more than this, brought De Gaulle back to power?

But back to my boys on Tenth Street—standing there in front of an elm tree, looking through the links of the fence on the back side of the Governor's mansion, filled with awe at what they were seeing. They stay in my mind because, you know, in this country, a long, stringy thirteen-year-old boy from somewhere could conceivably go to live in that big house. But if he should, if he ever does, it will be in part because there has not died out in his heart the ability to respond to the flags that wave around him. That is to say, he will have found something he can live by, he will have kept something he can still thrill to, for he has a long way to go.

What do you live by? What have you to remember? To what do you still respond? What waving flag in front of your eyes always brings a leap to your heart? What is there at the very center of your life about which you cannot get blasé? We have a long road ahead and need a lift of the heart.

REMOVE THAT THING

SOMEWHERE H. G. WELLS HAS REPEATED AN ANCIENT EASTERN STORY which stays in my mind. A prince fell in love with a very beautiful girl. All the people rejoiced that their prince had been blessed by such a perfect love. They rejoiced to see him united in marriage with this magnificent person; they basked in his great happiness.

His whole life revolved around his adoration for this girl and her almost total spiritual and physical perfection. Life for the prince became a thing of rare and total beauty. But to his terrible bereavement one day this beautiful rose petal, this one who was the center of his whole life, sickened and died. The young prince was bereft: he wept, he became ill, he lingered between life and death. The people waited with bated breath to see if their prince could recover. And eventually he did.

As an expression of this perfect love, this one holy thing he had known, this total adoration, this center of life, the prince resolved to build a perfect memorial. He sent craftsmen over the world to find the most perfect pieces of marble that could be found. On a wide plain surrounded by beautiful trees, he built in its very center the most magnificent shrine that he or any of his people had ever seen.

The prince found himself spending all the waking hours of his day outside the opening of this beautiful tomb. Its rose-colored marble matched in his memory the beauty of this wonderful one he had lost and he felt near her there. But after a while he began to feel that he had not done enough to express his love and adoration; so around the tomb he erected a beautiful shell of matching marble to try to say in an even more devoted way how wholly he had been committed to his love and adoration of this beautiful woman. The people came and admired and adored and joined the prince in his expression of his grief until this beautiful shell became inadequate to express the great adoration that still welled up in his heart. So over the beautiful tomb and the beautiful shell, he began the construction of a magnificent circle temple. It took years, millions of dollars, and the work of the best craftsmen in

44

the nation to complete over the tomb and the shell the magnificent circle temple that would enshrine forever his adoration.

One day the temple was completed. The prince sat for weeks, and then for months, in the nave of this magnificent temple. The people came, even from foreign countries, to see this most beautiful expression on earth of a man's love and adoration. But the prince was filled with despair: neither the tomb, nor the shell, nor the circle temple could do it. Over all this, he resolved to build the most magnificent building the whole world had ever seen. He impoverished himself; even his vast resources were not enough to bring from all the beautiful places of the world the things he wished to pile in a magnificent structure over the tomb and the shell and the circle temple. A great stone shroud, a high tower, the acme of all that the mind of man could devise in beauty at last was finished. And the prince, now an old man, walked across the archway that connected the high tower and this unbelievably beautiful stone shroud he had built as a memorial and stopped to look at the beauty. Far below him, a dark blob in the midst of all the beauty he had made, he spied the tomb that held the beauty he had loved. In a fit of petulance that there should be some blot or mar in all of his beauty, he said to his minions *"Remove that thing!"*

This man is legion. There are many who spend most of life trying to enshroud something treasured; then forfeit the treasure in the shroud built to display it.

A man can lose his calling as a public servant in his politics. I know men who have lost their home while building a house. People can lose their love in their attempt to decorate it and make it nice.

A man can lose his ministry altogether in its fringes. Called to give his mind, he winds up giving his legs running here and there, to and fro. A teacher can lose the content of his teaching in his efforts to acquire better techniques. Nations can lost their peace out of a justifiable concern with the techniques of protecting that peace.

This is a human problem: We are so made, I don't know why, that we spend most of our lives valuing the means more than the end. We have a certain moral set to our make-up, apparently, that means we are always putting more value on the tool than we are on the job it can do. We value the instrumental beyond the intrinsic. We worship the incidental and lose the eventual aim. Most commonly, we see this when marriage, the center of a man's life, gets lost in the economics of marriage. Sometimes, nearly always, a man runs the risk of losing his religious faith because he gets so wrapped up in its altar cloths, or its techniques, or its rituals, or its habits, or its institutional requirements. Therefore, he has always to keep cutting away at the things on the fringes of his life that threaten to make him call for the removal of the one thing he had set himself to preserve.

People lose character in the attempt to express their character. An education can get lost in extra curricula activities. Justice can get lost in the processes of justice. And parenthood can get lost in its own possessiveness.

Is Oscar Wilde right when he says, "Each man kills the thing he loves"? Does each man destroy the thing he loves by his frenzied desire to decorate it or protect it or defend it? Can a fellow see this, and can he change his way of life to where he no longer evaluates means over end, instrument over intrinsic, and the incident over the eventual? Can he get such a concept of marriage or religion or character or education that he quits running the daily risk of losing that which he loves?

"Remove that thing," the prince said. And it was what he had spent his life to keep.

BEGGARS IN VELVET

SOME OF THE MOST FAMOUS SERIOUS WRITINGS HAVE RECEIVED THEIR widest distribution as children's books. *Gulliver's Travels, Alice in Wonderland, Robinson Crusoe, Don Quixote,* and *Swiss Family Robinson* are not books for children. Every one of these is great social satire written only apparently for children. *Gulliver's Travels* is probably the most vicious antihuman document in English.

But notice the little nursery rhymes that your children know. These harmless jingles were all written to some specific situation, and many of them have sharp blows hidden within them. For example, "Little Miss Muffet," or "Mary, Mary, Quiet Contrary," or "Humpty Dumpty," or "Hey, Diddle, Diddle"; every one of these make a sharp thrust at some adult situation.

One I remember in particular:

> Hark, hark, the dogs do bark,
>   The beggars are coming to town,
> Some in rags,
>   Some in tags,
>   And some in velvet gowns.

47

Beggars in rags—they are real enough; their problems are real enough; their stories are true enough; their needs are real enough. We still see them in our culture. We usually help them. I have nothing to say of beggars in rags, though some are professionals. I have very little time to say anything about beggars in tags, though they are agile enough, and can usually hop around over most of life's situations. For beggars in tags have had to learn to make the remnants do.

Our worst shame in beggary is not beggars in rags; it is not even beggars in tags—our deep shame is the beggar who wears velvet gowns.

A beggar, whether he is in rags or tags or velvet gowns, is one who expects to get through, or by, or in, on another man's generosity. He expects to get what he needs on the basis of another man's work; he expects to be received into a particular fellowship on the basis of another man's contribution. I have some respect for velvet, and for gowns, but it is very hard for me to find any deep welling affection for the beggar in a velvet gown. And yet what tag is more expressive of our common situation than the phrase, "beggars in velvet"?

He is the special consideration man who always reminds you how he must be considered. This beggar in a velvet gown is the ineligible buyer who always expects to find things at a very special consideration; he is the tax squirmer—the fellow who literally would move out of the country, if he could, to keep from paying an honest tax. He is the special-pass man—he never had a legitimate ticket to anything in his life. On other levels, he may be an influence peddler, and he is almost always the sharp-corner man and the big-deal man. In his family relations, the word for him, whether the family ever says it or not, is niggardly. In his busi-

48

ness, at some time or other, and sometimes, most of the time, he is literally on the edge of felony. In his church, if he has a church and the strange thing about it is that most of these guys do have a church, the beggar in velvet is always the one who rides the contributions of the little old ladies and widows who out of their Social Security or their retirement far outgive him not only percentage wise, but in dollars and cents. His friends are made on the basis of their capacity to help him, for basically he is a contact man. He may be a preacher; he can also be a doctor, or a lawyer can be a beggar in velvet. A real-estate man, a retail man, a professor, or an agent of any kind—he can be anything, wealthy or not, and still be a beggar in velvet. In velvet or denim or a barrel, he is still a beggar.

He is always a sorry camper. Nobody would ever hunt with him twice. He is a sorry fellow to have with you on a mountain climb, because you couldn't afford to trust him on the other end of your rope. He is almost always an over-limit sportsman. He will have six or eight traffic tickets in his pocket because in traffic he is a three-hundred-horsepower bull.

What is the matter with him—this beggar in velvet? Usually he will tell you that he is a self-made man; but not always so. Sometimes he inherited not only his velvet, but also his awful beggary. He is a beggar, self-made or not. Basically and fundamentally, this fellow, this beggar in velvet, is a very hungry man; he has been hungry since he was a very small boy; and also he is a very immature man. He is a man who has almost no concept of the requirements of moral, social, political, economic manhood. The better word for it would be that he has no moral responsibility. You will have to watch out for him if you have to live with him. And if you do, I know only one from whom you can get the understanding and sympathy that will be required to see him through.

But do not mark him off. In this age of overvaluation of accessories and moral diffidence we are all so close to beggary that we dare not mark one another off. For we have our hungers too, and are not often averse to getting something for nothing as we can. "The beggars are coming," and are here, and in velvet. They are no longer monks and priests, as when the rhyme was written. There is more velvet now—and there are more beggars. This is the great moral threat in the velvet age.

II

THE WAY WE DO

THE PRESSURE COOKER

AT OBERLIN COLLEGE, BISHOP ANGUS DUN SAID THAT THE VAUNTED American melting pot is now a pressure cooker. It seems the idea is to cook our opinions down to an indistinguishable kind of hash. The vaunted American way of life becomes a kind of "pablum" that has no inconsistences, no lumps, and no contrary flavor. The great heresy—the greatest of heresies—is to disagree with anybody, but particularly to disagree with the majority. This is unforgivable; the unpardonable sin is to be different. You are not supposed to think differently; you are not supposed to express things differently, nor to read things differently; and there is a tragic development that means we ought not cut across traditional views. This means that even the professional historian must read things as favorable to the majority interpretation of our own situation.

At the University of Texas there teaches one of the most distinguished historians America has produced. Some months ago he released an article on the great American desert in which he said some things that are obviously true about deserts and their fringes. The howls that went up through the press would be laughable if this did not represent such a serious state of affairs. People simply do not like to face the truth since it means reading history and the future in a different light. The same great historian recently shared with me a scurrilous letter; it came from the pastor of some church in response to a paper given in Houston on the economic isolation of the South.

What is happening to us? This demand for conformity, this de-

53

mand for agreement, this demand for unanimity—is it really a demand for anonymity?

Amaury de Riencourt says that republics uniformly turn to the opposite of their original political views. The distinguished professor of modern history at Cambridge University, Herbert Butterfield, says that there is a gravitational pull in history itself which tends to bring down man's loftiest dreams. Over a span of time a long term purpose, a noble undertaking, a high principle generally manages to mix into itself a lot of earth. Martin Luther did not intend that his reformation principles should be so powerful in the rise of secular states, and the breakup and redistribution of wealth. The ideals of the French Revolution, so precious to Jefferson and the founders of our nation, have become the prop of rulers whose purpose it is to *strengthen* the power of existing government. Even the principle of revolution against oppression has become a means to re-creating new military power. When Bismarck supported universal suffrage his real goal was control of the lower classes in order to gain the strength that would beat off the middle classes who were opposed to him.

This business of high principles turning in on themselves and becoming their opposites is an historical illustration of Dostoevski's perpetual moral obliquity, for he describes how mankind seems always to wish to pervert these grand ideas as if we would cut them down to size. There is something within us that keeps pulling down our castles and pressing us into a dread unanimity which is really an anonymity. In the earliest days of our nation, when Virginia, North and South Carolina, Georgia, New York, and Massachusetts wished very desperately not to get into some binding agreement that would distort and destroy their existence as states, they hammered out the doctrine of States' rights. This was

always meant to be a brake against the absorption of the part totally in the whole. It was never meant to be a club for the preserva-
tion of provincial views. I sat at dinner recently with a lady who
is prominent in national party politics. She said that she really felt
as though she ought to whip me with her fists for expressing what
I had said on my telecast just before dinner. It was intolerable to
her that I should hold a different point of view on this matter of
States' rights.

Public education was a mighty dream, and still is, but it was never
meant to be a lever for the defense of the status of a certain section
of a population. The great ideal of intellectual freedom and personal
responsibility—this was never meant to be so twisted that it could
become a means of cloture of debate, or the means of stopping
freedom, or of denying responsibility. And yet, not so many days
ago when the brilliant and useful churchman, Joe Dawson, expressed his opposition to some pending legislation which I have
also opposed, the first thought of his adversary was, "What can we
find against this fellow that would smear him? Did he ever belong
to any front organizations?"

Many of those from whom we have learned would have been
ruined in the pressure cooker: Spinoza, Nietzsche, John Locke,
Heinrich Hiene would have found it impossible; Dostoevski,
Carlyle, Gibbon, Luther, and Kierkegaard just couldn't have made
it in a pressure cooker. The four great minds in America—Veblen,
Thoreau, Emerson, and Peirce gave up their jobs under pressures
from the system of things. As for Socrates; and Christ—*the Lord
Christ was crucified by the inversion of the great ideas of the culture
that produced him!*

In this modern melting pot some of us must preserve entity.
There is room always for what our British friends called "Her

Majesty's Loyal Opposition." Of one thing I am very sure, it is not time to cut off debate through our horror that anyone could possibly disagree with us. And of another thing I am very sure, that our whole country's future depends in vast measure on the ability of the common people to accept the reality and the necessity and the virtue of the fact that men shall be free to disagree.

WHAT THEY THINK

THE WAY I GET ALONG WITH MY NEIGHBORS IS DETERMINED NOT SO much by what I think of my neighbor as by what I think my neighbor thinks of me. Nearby, some boys from some of the so-called "best" families, broke over three-hundred windowpanes out of a new school building. Naturally the city authorities had all these sons from all these so-called "best" homes in custody, and the judge asked a famous psychologist to interview each boy separately. To the surprise of all concerned, he reported that no single boy approved the conduct of the group; on the contrary, every single boy in private interview expressed the firm conviction that he was the only one who thought it was bad conduct and that every other member of the group approved it, thought it was the thing to do, and was anxious to participate in it.

Many a youngster leaves home to go to school, finds himself in a new kind of gang, is anxious to fit in, is anxious to get along, and will therefore adopt a pattern of conduct or a way of living that his code does not approve simply because he thinks it is what the others think is the thing to do. Not that he is weak—it is that we are all largely motivated by what we think other people think. Now this motivation on the basis of what we think others think has disastrous consequences. I think any person in my calling could name fifty young couples who live a masquerade. Their living habits are not at all representative of their inmost convictions, their childhood rearing, their deepest impression of what makes life worth living, or their highest values; but they are motivated to live on this level because of what they think others think is the thing to do.

One of the big factors in domestic inability to live up to our codes lies in what the husband secretly thinks his wife thinks and vice versa. These secret thoughts about each other motivate a great deal of the misconduct and produce situations of domestic discord. It is beginning to appear that much more important than the factor of what I think secretly of my wife, or what my wife thinks of me, is what I think she thinks of me and vice versa. Not what I think of my wife, but what my wife *thinks I think*. This has a very wide possibility of application. It opens up an explanation of other areas within which trouble comes.

This is particularly true in the matter of religious conviction. Many a person has never given any honest expression of his own deep inner religious and moral convictions simply because he is shut off by his dependence on what he thinks others think about such convictions or such opinions. It also works with respect to a philosophy of life. Whole areas of life are shut off from our investigation simply because we think those around us think that to inquire too much about life's mysteries like birth and death and the infinite are beyond us and therefore we pretend to content ourselves rather happily and from a very shallow viewpoint with life's inconsequentials. We go through a whole lifetime underrating our own capacities for life's heaviest burdens, life's heaviest concerns, life's most valid values.

This works viciously at the level of social action our time demands and produces mass cowardice. Many men have convictions that are liberal and free, but will not express them because of what they think others think. If on some occasion one is goaded into a forthright expression of a thing in which he knows himself to be right he is utterly amazed at the kind of people, at the number of people, who will say to him, "I wish I had said that, I have felt that way about it a long, long time." But because we are so dependent upon what we think others think about things, we live very timidly.

In *Tomorrow Is Forever* a man who was seriously disfigured in World War I had been a refugee from home for twenty years in Austria. At the beginning of World War II he was assigned to his old plant, his own chemical company, for work producing penicillin. His wife, to whom he had never revealed himself because of his horrible disfigurement, had married the new president of the company. Her son by the first husband had grown to manhood and wanted to go into World War II. The old crippled chemist, actually the father of the boy, knows of the mother's awful fear of war and grief over her husband, but sent the boy to fight, saying, *"Every man opposes the evil in his own time, or else he accepts it."* Every man has the obligation to follow the highest code he knows in opposing the evil in his own time, or else he accepts the evil! There is a vast difference between the code most of us have and the way we follow it and express it. We ought not to be intimidated by what we think our friends will think about us.

THE TRANSFER OF RESENTMENT

Down the street I have a couple of neighbors with whom I don't get on so well. One is a fox terrier and the other is a shepherd dog. Ordinarily they are very well behaved good neighbors, but they have one very interesting trait in common. They will lie for hours—one right next to the curb with his nose just over our property line, and the terrier behind a bush fifty yards or so farther down the street, waiting for my car to start. So far as I know mine is the only car they chase. They are always there. Sometimes when I am coming home late I forget them and am startled half out of my wits by a wild rush from off to the left. With their ruff up, their eyes wild, and all the fanfare you can imagine, they give me a flying, dashing, snarling escort all the way to the corner.

I have tried to analyze this particular enmity—my car is no older than many on our block; and I don't think it is a bit noisier than some on our street. I have never had any particular disaffection for these neighbors; I have never harmed them. I just couldn't figure out for a long time why they chased my car, why they always chased it, and why they did not seem particularly to resent any other car on the block. Finally, I figured it out. They just don't like my old red setter. He is too big for them. Because they don't like him, they have transferred their resentment to the automobile that I drive. They get a charge out of that resentment. It has sparked up their whole lives; they have come to live just to express their resentment of that old red dog by committing assault and battery on my automobile. It is the most human trait I have ever seen in animals.

Most of us do it. Most of us do it some way or another. Certainly not in chasing any particular automobile up and down the street until we are nearly frantic with joy and hate, but we do it in one way or another.

Resentments of one kind or another are native to human beings. It would be an error to say that human beings are not supposed to have resentments. They are native to us. It would be serious if a child did not learn to hate certain things. In fact, as Karl Menninger says it, "A child comes into the world already equipped with the capacity for hatred, and this he learns to use, and he learns to use it either wisely or unwisely." He learns in his mere infancy that he must have a dislike for, or in fact a resentment against, or in stronger words a hatred of certain things that will harm him. And his resentment (or his hatred) becomes the means of self-preservation. The trouble lies not so much in the fact that we are capable of hating, but that our hatred or resentment gets out of focus. When it is misfocused, it becomes a deadly dissipator of happiness; then it becomes a deadly destroyer loose in our lives to warp, twist, wreck, and maim the lives around us. Like the pups down the street, we are particularly guilty of transferring our resentment to some safer object.

Now the common objects of transferred resentment I think you would recognize. There are whole families that seem to focus resentments of each other on a certain child. There are men I know who have managed to pile all the failures and resentments in their own lives on to some particular institution. There are those who will place on a wife or on a husband their resentments within the neighborhood or within their church or within their job or within their own social strata. In-laws are particularly subject to receiving this kind of resentment, so is religion, and so is government.

I have a friend whom I had not seen for twenty years or more. I visited him a couple of summers ago and noticed as we talked through the evening that every resentment he had had twisted itself and now was focused on what he called "chain banking." If he went into the store to buy an item and it was two cents higher than it had been the day before, the blame was focused on the chain banks. He had transferred all his resentments on his job as a railroad man, all his resentments as a citizen, to the banks that operate up and down the Coast. A friend of mine tells me that the family can't convince his father that the No. 2 can from a chain store is not smaller than the No. 2 can that he used to get from his neighborhood grocery. They even take identical cans from different stores and show him that they are the same size, and he will still keep his resentment by claiming that certain firms don't fill their cans quite as full as another firm.

One of the keenest expressions of this transfer of resentment is the anti-Semitic form of race prejudice. This kind of transference appears where we categorize and stereotype and try to treat all people of a certain group as if they were all just exactly alike. I have known people who will transfer all their resentments of local situations and tensions to a vague entity that we style "Washington." I have known a man to focus all his resentments of his long life of neglect, abandon, and separation from the church on one pastor whom he could not find at a particular moment that he wanted him. I think the most common expression of this transference occurs in the phrase, "that woman." Usually when you hear it, it is a child who is focusing all his resentment on his mother, or it is some husband who is focusing all his resentment of himself against his wife.

The most tragic kind of transfer occurs when a man's resentment is not against his employer, or his friends, or anything tangible in his own area, but is a hidden inner hatred for himself. Many times such a man will focus his resentment against that most intimate group with which he lives, his own family, and life will literally become a terror; simply because he has transferred his resentment of himself to the group with whom he is most intimately situated.

Every day, if you will watch for it, you can see a man express his resentment against something—an incident in a store, against a mail box by the way he flips up and down the lever on the open lid, or the way he slams the door of his automobile, or the door of his house. Everyday job tensions, personal tensions, are expressed against inanimate objects, or what is worse, against other people. More of this happens in traffic than anywhere else—a man who has had a bad day at the office or a bad day on the job gets in this five o'clock pell-mell of ours and he becomes a holy terror to try to get along with at a stop light or at any intersection.

Some resentments are native to us—we need them. They act for our self-preservation. But transferred to objects that are not to blame they become self-destructive. I can't explain this to the little fox terrier—I don't think he would understand me. I can't make it clear to that shepherd dog who gets such a charge out of chasing me off down the street—I don't think he would understand either. But I can make it clear to me: A prejudiced man is a man who cannot change his mind about his resentments. Don't get in position where your resentments cannot be changed—focus your resentments where they belong.

THE TRANSFER OF EXPERTNESS

JUST ANY OLD MAGAZINE IN YOUR HOUSE WILL AFFORD SOMEWHERE in its ads an illustration of the way we transfer expertness. It is one of the most ludicrous things we do. All human beings seem to have the capacity for accepting the word of an expert outside his field of expertness. We create illegitimate authority. We assume that because a fellow develops a capacity, or skill, or gift in one direction that he is qualified to give us direction in some other field.

Why should I ask a first baseman what kind of *razor* to use? A barber would be better. Why should I consult a rodeo-roping expert about the *engine oil* I am going to use? A mechanic knows more. Any four or five-year-old boy would be better qualified to tell me how good a certain kind of *candy bar* is than Buffalo Bill.

A little friend of mine is a football enthusiast. I asked her who was the best football player in her room. She told me, but I questioned her judgment unwisely and she clenched the matter with, "Of course he is the best football player in our room, his mother flies an airplane."

Sometimes on a committee you see a particular example of this: I recall with enjoyment the fellow who owned a gang of oil wells and had real skill in handling his estate. But he turned up overnight as an expert on stained-glass windows and religious symbolism. It was simply that the whole committee assumed that because he could get money together he could also put stained glass together in proper proportions.

On a certain university faculty a physicist developed tremendous influence as a man of religion. The only thing wrong with his influence was that it was tight, narrow, squeezing, and legalistic, a law-centered thing like his physics. It was incapable of doing anything in the way of lifting lives, and all he could do was tie youngsters into tighter knots emotionally.

The fact that a man is a great wheel in the nylon sock business does not qualify him per se to lead a seminar in Christian love. The fact that a man knows law does not qualify him to be his own plumber. The fact that a man knows medicine does not qualify him anywhere else of itself. Community is not achieved on the basis of knowledge alone. But we do this to people—we keep imposing on innocent people an expertness most of them would not claim. We keep expecting that certain gifts that have worked in one direction will just automatically transfer over into another field. We respect a man in science when he will speak in theology; we respect the opinion of a man in medicine when he will speak in business, though not vice versa, I assure you.

Once the source of social power was property. This is where nobility came from in the first place. The power to control land and property created nobility. But the years came and went, and knowledge came to be a most important source of power. A man who had know-how had power though sometimes he was a slave. Skills, the ability to work with materials, and property created a great middle class of people, and power began to come to them. But any time we transfer this power out of its native realm we are creating for ourselves an illegitimate kind of authority. Haven't you known some fathers who were experts with everything? It just can't be—a man just can't be an expert in anything and everything.

It is bad enough for us to do this to people by imposing expertness on them, but it is worse when this fellow on whom we impose that authority accepts our transfer as if it were true. When he himself, in a very subtle way, begins to assume that because he is pretty sharp in this area he must be pretty smart over here, too, then he betrays himself into an incompetence. Here and there, throughout our community there are people like this; certain physicians, certain pastors, certain businessmen, certain public-spirited people whom we cause to betray themselves into incompetence simply by depending upon them too much. It is bad when a man is teased into assuming that he has an authority or knowledge or an expertness that he hasn't got. This is illustrated any time a pastor is tempted to play doctor—he is not qualified to be a doctor. It is illustrated any time a pastor is tempted to act like a psychiatrist—he is not a psychiatrist and he has no right to try to take the place of one. All he can hope to do is to qualify himself so that he may recognize when the services of such highly trained men are needed. There are dangers involved in our accepting an authority to which we are not entitled.

Community itself occurs best when each man comes into his own best and his own highest. And right here obtrudes the meaning of intellectual humility. It helps a man arrive at that level of ethics where he is very careful what he marks off, and who he marks off. He is very careful what he lumps together as being a valid generalization. He learns not to give expertness to people when it is not deserved. And he learns not to take authority that isn't due. Community does not depend on knowledge; it depends on an honest and valid intellectual humility that will allow a man to accept what all the other members of the community have to give.

Our greatest teacher, Jesus Christ, never allowed himself to be drawn outside his area. They tried to trap him once to make him sound like a politician; in other instances they tried to make him sound like a priest; he always stayed in the area he knew—love, and a man's relationship with his Heavenly Father.

TROUBLE IS PEOPLE

FOLKS ARE ALMOST NEVER FUSSING ABOUT WHAT THEY SAY THEY ARE fussing about. The husband says he doesn't like the coffee this morning but he may not have coffee in mind at all; he may be saying that he doesn't like his wife or his boss. People dress up their dislikes and frustrations to protect ego. Sometimes they pick up banners and wave them and get on opposite sides of some ideological controversy for very personal reasons. A man just doesn't like this other guy and therefore he will support most any opposing view. Sometimes he tries to do this in a very respectable way, and always he tries to do it in a very inobvious way. But there is a fundamental personal dislike that puts people on opposite sides. Sometimes the sides of a controversy are really quite close together.

We have read for years about factions within major political parties. There is very little fundamental difference between the opposing factions in these political situations. At bottom, four or five people just happen not to like four or five people.

Great ideological differences developed between Jefferson and Hamilton. But long before Alexander Hamilton's federalist notion had come to its full supremacy, and long before Thomas Jefferson's ideas of democracy were completely formed, these two fellows just did not like each other. It is quite clear now that General Grant had a great deal more regard for General Lee than he had for some of his own associates. Even though he placed General W. F. (Baldy) Smith in command of an army and then moved him before he could actually take command, his resentment was not against Smith; his trouble was with Butler!

Here are a couple of competing firms. There is no personal liking between the heads of those firms. If a man is not of the highest character he may begin to credit his opponent with dishonesty or inferior business ethics; at bottom it may be simply a resentment that the other fellow is in business.

At bottom most ideological enmity is personal and begins in some slight, insult, or fancied wrong. Ideas do not fight. People fight with ideas. Ideas are not active; ideas are passive. There are opposite notions but they do not oppose themselves on their own accord, for ideas have no will, no power of action. Ideas are used to fight with by people, and occasionally someone will pick up an old idea that is really an accusation and bop somebody over the head with it. At bottom the fundamental problem is not loyalty to the idea as much as it is dislike for the other person.

A young presbyter, Arius, trained in the school of Antioch, came down to Alexandria to preach. He was an imposing and rather handsome fellow, something of a withdrawn, ascetic, would-be-scholar type. He was not as smart as he thought he was, but he represented the great school at Antioch and he would let no one in Alexandria forget it. His rise in Alexandria was not as rapid as he expected. When the young Alexander was made Bishop of the Christian churches in Alexandria, he called the clergy together for one of his famous theological lectures. Someone asked Arius how he liked it; and Arius said, "Well, I came down here from Antioch thinking I was going to hear some great teachers and some great preachers around Alexandria but they are all about like the run of the mill over at Antioch. As a matter of fact, I thought the Bishop sounded a little bit tritheistic."

Now it so happened that Alexander was touchy; he had worked hard to bring Greek distinctions into his attempts to speak about the oneness and the threeness of God. He considered himself horribly insulted by what Arius had said, and Arius had felt himself horribly abused by the way the Alexandrians had treated him. They could not afford to fight over who could preach the best;

they couldn't afford to let ego show; they could not afford to admit that their trouble was that Arius had said that most anybody at Antioch could preach better than this. They had to use ideological labels to make their fight respectable, and the fight was on. Before it was over (if it is over) it involved a whole empire; it involved all of Christendom, and not even the death of Constantine, after he had called three synods to try to stop it, could stop it. Arius died, and this didn't stop it because Athanasius, who had come to succeed Alexander, claimed God had slapped Arius dead in a public rest room because of his theological views. For at least three more centuries the fight was hot, and to this day you can get a discussion in any pastors' conference I know about the difference between the Alexandrian view and the Arian view.

Now there was content to the view of Arius, of course; there was theological content to the view of Alexander; but this was not fundamental in the beginning. Arius died, and Athanasius died—they are all dead; but underneath eighteen centuries, some men just didn't like one another.

Be careful what banner you wave. Someone may foist on you some ideological banner to wave in their fight just because they happen not to like some other people. And in your own quarrels forego that idiotic practice of trying to make a silly little personal fight seem as if it were representing some deep and important world view when it doesn't. Ideas do not fight; people use them as clubs to represent their personal differences and to keep from seeming small in the personality conflicts that mark marriage, church, university, politics, and business.

The amazing thing is that we can get so proud of ourselves about the ideas that we pick up to use as clubs in some fray with our neighbors. The whole thing could usually be fixed by an admission of one's own shallowness. But most of us are willing to be involved as heavyweights in what is really a lightweight encounter.

Folks almost never fuss about what they say they are fussing about—it is not ideas, it is people who make conflict.

BLIND LOYALTIES

Any serious-minded man concerned with the good or the bad of things must sometime make a stand where he is. If a man stands where he is on the basis of wrong loyalties he may wind up with an ungodly use of a good principle. What is worse, if he gives himself blindly to his loyalties, he may wind up with an ungodly kind of God. He may become so involved in something that has a good sound that he does not see how far he is from the true right or wrong of the situation.

Lord Chesterton used to say that for a man to cry, "My country, right or wrong," was about the same as, "My mother, drunk or sober!" That is to say, a man who lives by an emotional loyalty may find himself so involved in a set of ungodly propositions that he may as well have no loyalties at all. This is the kind of emotional malady that turns a beautiful little high-school teenager into a spitting cat that you have seen pictured in the current school crises.

Any loyalty, in any kind of world, needs to be weighed in the light of a man's highest loyalty. If you are Jewish or if you are Christian, you have a very clear saying as to what your highest loyalty involves. It comes out of the Jewish tradition. It is the greatest contribution of the Jewish faith: "Hear, O Israel: the Lord thy

God is One Lord: And thou shalt love the Lord thy God with all thine heart, and with all thy soul, and with all thy might." By this principle a man weighs every loyalty.

But he is very quickly aware of a whole procession of intermediate rights, principles, or authorities that reside somewhere between his individual rights and that due this great God whom he is called to love. That is to say, there are rights of an individual, rights of a municipality, rights of a state; rights of a nation; of a hemisphere; of a whole world, and a world government. He knows the authority of the human race, but *he has no right at any point in that procession of powers to use any intermediate right as if it were an ultimate right!* He has no right to invoke the power of States' rights if it is in support of what is in itself an ungodly and wrong thing. *Nor must he invoke any political, and therefore partial, right to countenance a moral wrong.* The tragedy of States' rights is connected with its immoral usage. There is no question about the power, or even the rightness, or even the desirability of local determination. What is questionable is the use of this given power, this constitutional power of local determination, of States' rights, or local government *to control or effect or produce a situation that is filled with moral wrong.*

This is why a man must examine his loyalties; he must know that his loyalties are not blind loyalties. He must know that his support of these rights is not based on a moral wrong. He must be sure that his fidelity to lesser values does not cut across the highest loyalty of his which begins, "Thou shalt love the Lord thy God with all thine heart, and with all thy soul, and with all thy might."

Sometimes the exercise of political powers, of these intermediate rights, or these personal powers, can be such as to cause a man to deny the whole race. Sometimes he gets caught in an emotional outburst, his picture gets in the paper, and he looks like something hardly human at all.

I have rejoiced in the courage, and in the open-eyed loyalty of this strange and splendid man, Brooks Hays. I heard him speak of the agony in Little Rock before about eight thousand men—"We have extremists, we have reactionaries, we have violent men, but these are not Christian men." That is to say, these are not men who are following their highest loyalty. A man cannot be obedient to this highest loyalty and invoke an intermediate loyalty in the name of what is essentially an immoral or an ungodly treatment of other human beings. This is the effect of blind loyalties. Intermediate powers have in themselves great good, but they must be invoked in the name of the good for the whole.

WITHIN THE MAN

I STUCK OUT MY HAND TO ACKNOWLEDGE MY INTRODUCTION TO ONE of the local denizens. He reluctantly offered his hand, and said, "I suppose you are like all the rest." "Like all the rest of what?" And he said, "Preachers!"

On a bus I heard a woman say, "Well, what do you expect from an insurance company?" On a street corner in Washington I heard, "They are all just alike, whether it is Oregon, Illinois, Washington, or Alabama. All politicians are just alike."

The first of the week, at one of the local hospitals, I heard a woman customer talking about the medical profession, and what she said I am not going to repeat. A couple of weeks ago a man in a drugstore was piling the whole legal profession in one basket and throwing it down the drain. I have heard the same thing done to the Air Force, university students, teenagers, and female women of the opposite sex.

Whether you deal with ministers, insurance brokers, senators, doctors, lawyers, Air Force folks, university folks, teenagers, or female women folks, people who discard us all on the basis of a bad experience with one are guilty of the sorriest, most unreasonable kind of emotional nonthinking. Bad categorization leads to prejudiced living anywhere. Certainly, there are sorry preachers, just as there are sorry plumbers, just as there are sorry citizens. Even some good ones go sour, but it is a vicious kind of nonthinking that dumps the whole category out the window on the basis of a bad experience with one.

The sources of morality, the springs of goodness or badness are not in the ministry, not in the insurance companies, not in the Senate, not in the medical profession, or the legal profession, or the Air Force, or the university, or a teenage group. The sources of morality are not a man's profession. The springs of our morality are deeper than our professional calling. By being a lawyer, by being a minister, by being a doctor, by being a senator, a man assumes the burden of the guilt of the whole calling. I will grant you this. But in so far as being a source of morality is concerned, the ministry, the political calling, or that of medicine, or that of law, these things are impotent to determine a man's morality. The state, for example, cannot determine the goodness or the badness of the men who say they serve it. The springs of morality are deeper.

Left alone, apart from any calling, without some hand that shapes and lifts and moves, men and women will go on as usual—as Bernard Bell says, trying to get something for nothing. Each will try to make another work for his own benefit. Cornering wealth, and looking for privilege, and buying dear and selling high, cutting moral corners on one wheel, two timing and lying and mixing noble dreams and dreadful monkeyshines, killing the prophets and later building cathedrals for them; gullibly following in and out of war, because the human being who has lost his bearings becomes victim to his own delusions and begins to spread abroad his false categorizations as if this would fix things.

So one says, "A preacher didn't tell me the truth once," and he marks off a great group of noble, fairly intelligent, and honest men. Or a man hears of something that has gone sour in a business firm and he tries to mark off a whole category; or a man knows of one or two or ten in public life who are false, and therefore will, with one foul swoop, mark off all men who are trying to do an honest and a desperately needed kind of thing.

The sources of morality, I say, are not in a man's profession. And if you have decent thinking power at all, and are able to be more than emotional about any kind of thinking, you do not casually mark off a whole calling, a whole category, or a whole race. Man must stand on his own feet. In so far as morality is concerned, goodness and badness do not belong to the profession, race, or to any other category. They belong to the man, and he has within himself the springs of morality to which he can respond, or which he can cut off and smother and thereby become something beyond the pale of capacity for human service. None of us is like all the rest. For all the rest are not alike. And we have to learn sooner or later that the springs are deeper. Goodness or badness is not in the State, and goodness or badness is not in the profession; goodness and badness reside in the man.

OUR TIGHT LITTLE ISLANDS

JUST SO LONG AS WE SIT ON OUR OWN TIGHT LITTLE ISLANDS, BEHIND a façade of our own desire for isolation within our own culture— just as long will surliness, fear, and resentment eat at us. A people which will not separate itself from its tight little islands is a people

David H. C. Reid, once Chaplain at Edinburgh, described a young

We have no right to such islands.

David H. C. Reid, once Chaplain at Edinburgh, described a young pastor who was building the ideal church and manse. His church would sit here, and his manse would sit there. He would have his study in the manse and his pulpit in the church connected by a sealed corridor—a zealous wife would guard the door. There would be no telephone—his existence would be hermetically sealed through the week with his clean and chaste theology books. And then on Sundays he would erupt from the study door, dash along the corridor and into the pulpit. Nothing would have bothered him, nothing would have upset him, all he would have to do is preach. His gospel would be chaste, pure, and untrammeled with the world, that is quite true, but how out of touch with things that matter. When asked how he liked his new parson, an old Scot said that he supposed he was all right, in the main, but six days he was invisible and the seventh day he was incomprehensible. It just won't work to shut ourselves off on these tight little islands.

I have never been quite comfortable with a man in an office who always has a perfectly clean desk. There is something a little too sterile about it. He is too well caught up on his work and it could mean that he is not participating, he is not in contact, he is not involved with enough unfinished things in his life.

If you live on a tight little island you miss the whole universe that is living and throbbing around you. Wolfgang Goethe agonized to produce his immortal *Faust* while he was administrator for a school district consisting of thousands of children. Frail, large-domed, bandy-legged little Sören Kierkegaard forsook every day the great house in Copenhagen where he was hammering out his existentialism through the hours of the night and the early morning. Every day he came out to prowl the flower markets and stalls of downtown Copenhagen. Perhaps you knew that Karl Marx wrote his *Das Kapital* on an old dining-room table on which there was seldom if ever enough to eat. Eleven children ran in and out that dining room and around that table while he worked. Potty, ugly Socrates bumbled around the market places of Athens. While the great Fëdor Dostoevski was prisoner in a Siberian barracks he worked with frozen fingers at the scraps of paper that later would become a great book. There is no valid contribution to my culture made without my participation.

At the little movie house we headed for on Saturday afternoons there was a section called the "peanut gallery." Most of us young riffraff hit for that. We could sit in the peanut gallery and make remarks, and shoot with the hero or the villain, and scream with those who were caught and throw our peanut hulls over the brass rail that separated us from the floor below; but we were not involved in anything; we knew we were perfectly safe in the balcony. There are no valid peanut galleries in our time. A man cannot live a sterile, antiseptic, withdrawn life; it isn't life, and it is not living.

All of us need our moments for solitude. But sometimes we have to learn to pray while we go, to create as we sweep by, and to meditate between the acts. A man who would live in this frenzied time without being himself in a frenzy must learn that life has room enough for solitude, and creation, but much of one's solitude is caught in a crowd. We ought not overlook the creative potential of a busy life. All of us look for a tight little island. Even Jeremiah wanted to find a wilderness inn away from the crossroads where he could be alone for a while. All mothers with children know what I am talking about. All of us look for a tight little island, but nothing really creative, nothing really contributive to our time can come wholly out of isolation. It has to come out of participation.

We need to be reminded of the surliness of loneliness. Haven't you seen, in your own neighborhood, some once well-made home, some once well-made couple, turn into examples of isolation, surliness, and loneliness? Sometimes we are inclined to say it is because they have no children. But there are other people's children. People get afraid on their tight little islands. People grow surly on their tight little patios. Move on to the mainland. There is no valid contribution to be made to our culture that does not involve participation. There are no valid islands any more—not for withdrawal from life. Our time is too needful; hearts of people are too hungry. Men have to learn not to live in a frenzy in the midst of a frenzied time. There are no tight little islands. There is no valid contribution to be made without being involved in the needs and agonies and strains of one's own city. Find the area where you belong and participate.

UNSUITED FOR THE TRAFFIC

ON THE ROAD TO DALLAS I SPOTTED AN UNUSUAL HITCHHIKER. HE WAS clad for travel all right, but under his left arm he was carrying something I never saw a hitchhiker bother to carry. It was a pair of skates attached to a set of fancy shoes. He stood there, thumbing a ride with a kind of winsome look on his face and that foolish pair of skates under his arm.

I worried about that fellow—if no ride came, would he try to skate to Dallas? A ride might be difficult to get; and so he had a form of transportation with him. Did he know the inadequacies of this form or transportation, or was he carrying along a hobby not intended for this traffic? He did have alternatives—he might get a ride; he could walk; and if he had to, where the road was paved, he could skate.

As I watched that fellow out of sight in the rearview mirror I asked again, "Why do we cling to our old neighborhood notions, our old outworn race concepts, our own out-paced ideas of what truly constitutes progress when the traffic of real progress is so heavy around us?" Most of us keep a set of old skates that we carry under our arm on our long road; it is a hobby we ride, or a sub-stitute we cherish, or an alternative we cling to. But many of our ideas are unsuited for the traffic around us.

For nearly eight hundred years the traffic has been toward equality of opportunity for all men. Though not automatic, the progress has been uninterrupted, even if impeded. In the eleventh century there was no way any other than a noble could be a noble. In the thir-teenth century you could buy nobility at a fairly low price in France. Even the political maneuverings of the powerful medieval Church worked to equalize men in that men who had no land could on the ladder of the Church come into positions of power and influence. The tyrannies and vices of kings worked in behalf of equality. Every personal property right wrested from the landed families was a step in the direction of equality for all men. The day the peasant stood and closed a clod of dirt in his hand, squeezed it, dropped it to the ground, and swore undying loyalty to the lord who owned that land was a day that was beginning to pass. Every new market, every new idea, every new discovery, every craving, every major event for seven hundred years has worked in the direction of opportunity for all men. Why do we keep carrying, I say, our little pair of skates under our arms as if we might, by using that substitute, come away from the danger of really seeing all men equal?

The Crusades covered a wild two hundred years when men moved on the new Jerusalem as if it were heaven itself. It is awfully hard to find much good coming out of the Crusades except that the absence of the great landowners from England and France and Germany and Italy meant the breakdown of vital feudalistic principles; and the peasants who tilled that land gradually began to come into possession of that land; not to mention the lessons that Saracens taught the nobles.

Every great invention of the last seven or eight hundred years has pushed us closer to the ultimate goal of opportunity for all men. The Colt .44 revolver that western men carried was affectionately called, was it not, the equalizer? When firearms first became widely used, they were one of the most powerful forces of the time for the equalizing of men. Up until this time when men went into battle, the men who had horses and armor around them, coats of mail, and so on, were the nobles who could afford them. And the poor vassals who surrounded those horses—thirty or forty to the horse usually—had no possibility of being equal to Sir whatever-his-name-was who owned a mighty war horse. But any sort of peasant looking across the barrel of any kind of blunderbuss became the equivalent, the equal, even the superior of any kind of man on any kind of horse.

The discovery of America led to a vast experiment in the equality of opportunity for all mankind. I guess we might call it a holy experiment. Much has been wrong with America, with the United

States, and our heritage. But notice this: no government of the United States has ever been overthrown, or a new regime instituted, by the army, or the navy, or an armed revolt—all our transitions have always come at the polls except where there has been a rare assassination; and in no case of assassination has any introduction of new elements in political power come into government. There is still a mighty hope that this holy experiment will be used in the direction of the increase of opportunity if our citizens can be brought to throw away their old outmoded hobbies, their old outmoded forms of social transportation.

The current situation all over the world—French Morocco, South Africa, Central Africa, Indo-China—wherever the news cameras go, the current situation is such that the world knows that men twist and turn and writhe in a furor of desire for room to live. It is not new, it is old. And de Tocqueville, in *Democracy in America,* more than a hundred years ago gave a solemn warning that society changes its forms, humanity changes its condition, new destinies are always impending; the gradual though always impeded development of the principle of equality is a fact—it goes on now; it seems durable. It is not an automatic progress but events, as well as men, contribute to its progress.

Would it be wise to imagine that a social movement, the causes of which lie so far back, can be checked by the efforts of any one segment of population in a generation? Can it be believed that democracy which has overthrown the feudal system and vanquished kings will retreat before tradesmen and capitalists?

A hundred and twenty years ago men were talking like this, and the fever has spread, and men everywhere wish to be free. We can help it along by throwing away the skates—the old ideas that we keep cluttering around us along the way the traffic is moving.

Or we can be left alone on the highway to follow as best we can. I know progress is not automatic. But I know too that even the "wrath of men" sometimes serves good ends.

THE POWER OF OLD EXPLOSIVES

NORTH OF THE CITY OF SEOUL THERE ARE OLD EXPLOSIVES ALMOST ANY-where you go away from the main paths. For a long time the 440th Aviation Construction Battalion camped in a mountain pocket infested with old explosives. There were crews of demolition experts combing the country side and little off-the-way roads for land mines and other explosives that had been left there by the Communists or by our own forces. All through the day you could hear old ammunition being blown up in the demolition dump across the hills. One day during my visit thirty men fresh from the States were brought in, issued equipment, briefed on their mission. The briefing officer did not mention the demolition crews hard at work across the hill. Just as he finished his address a five-hundred pounder went off, the smoke and rubble flew up in the air, and came rolling over the hill. There wasn't a whole man in sight! There were feet sticking out from under trucks, and feet sticking up from piles of sandbags. There were mess kits and blankets and all sorts of paraphernalia strewn all over the lot, and the few faces that I could see sticking out from under trucks had awful surprise written on them—as if they were saying, "We thought the war was over!"

The effect of old explosives is not always so comical. You learn to walk gingerly and carefully, as if on eggs, alongside an escort who knows the way when you are going through that kind of country. Old explosives are dangerous.

During the Korean war our forces sowed the country down with seventy-two-hour fused demolition bombs. The Communists learned to screw a clamp on these bombs containing a strong spring. They would attach a long cord, jerk the fuse past the point of explosion, take the fuse out, refuse the bomb, and *use our own demolition bomb against us.*

Most of us do this in different ways almost as deadly. In a hundred ways married people use old explosives against themselves. Here our prejudices become most deadly. Every old dud can become a booby trap. Years ago you made some unfortunate business move, and this old explosive goes off again every pay day. Driving your husband's car you lose $140 worth of fender, shall we say. Since then every drive has been a torture for he keeps dragging out that old explosive and it goes off right at you. The pace your neighbors set can be an old explosive, some petty but nerve-racking habit— like how long it takes you to wash for a meal. Such can be a sputtering fuse threatening to blow up twenty years of married life. Perhaps you are a housekeeper who has an inordinate regard for the details of housekeeping; you want the "antimacassars" just so; you want everything kept straight, and you have forgotten that homes and houses are made to live in. There can be a crackling of machine gun fire over this all through a lifetime. Maybe there is some particular foible or trait of weakness or fear. If you will just play on it right you can make marriage a hell on earth. Sometimes a man runs across some old dud that his wife knew years before— one can make a fine explosion out of this.

In some moment of weakness he told you about some early indiscretion, or perhaps she confessed some real mistake of hers, and it keeps coming out of the corner. Maybe there was a former marriage—this begins to get serious! Perhaps there are children by a previous marriage, and every crisis that comes up sees this as part of the explosion. Perhaps he has committed some grievous wrong and has confessed it. It has supposedly been forgiven but it comes up everytime there is a family discussion. A woman can flail a man to death with old explosives. A man can tear the spirit out of any marriage—with ghosts—ghosts that shouldn't have been allowed to stay alive at all. They are there in the closet all the time, like an old bazooka shell, waiting for someone to hammer on the fuse.

Love means, in this context, "don't hammer on the fuse." Forgiveness means "sealed off," "forgotten," "never to be referred to again." Marriage ought to mean disarmament.

Paul Tillich in *Love, Power, and Justice* says that love is the desire that maintains between separation and reunion. And the object of love is for us to come together. If the meaning of love is separation and reunion, the meaning of forgiveness is simply this: it won't explode again. Perhaps, at your house, there ought to be some old explosives removed never to be referred to again. For forgiveness means: it won't explode again.

THE PANIC BUTTON

"To hit the panic button," has become a general term for any situation where a fellow comes unglued in the middle. Actually it refers to the warning signal a pilot sounds when his craft is in trouble and the crew must evacuate by parachute. "To hit the panic button," means to use the last door, to go out the last window, to use the only opening left to you. It refers to the ultimate in decision.

Most human relationships are wired for panic too; but we often hit the panic button too soon. This is why we drop so many courses; this is the reason we do many wrong things. This is a reason why so many people move so often from one town to another. This is the reason back of many resignations. This is why separation comes so often in young marriages. This is one reason for needless divorces.

When the tappets in the engine of your new automobile begin to "ping" you don't jump out of the automobile to save your life. When the tube burns out in the television set you don't junk the set. When the baby gets dirty you don't throw it away and hope for another. But in vital relationships people hit the panic button all too soon. After six months of marriage you simply cannot say yet whether or not you are incompatible! After the first bad report it may be too soon to say, "I'm out of the insurance business." The first time you are on scholastic probation is too early to drop out of school because you decide you have no ability. We hit the button too soon!

Recently I was in a squadron equipment room shortly after the commander of that squadron was forced to leave his jet fighter to crash in a rice paddy. The hydraulic system on his aircraft went out when the pumps disintegrated. There was no alternate system of manual control available to him. The major described how he took his check list out of his pocket, went down the list to see if there was anything that he could do; notified the other pilots that he was leaving the flight; notified radio control that he was leaving the craft at six thousand feet; turned everything he needed to turn, rechecked his list; waited until the plane came from eighteen thousand feet to six thousand feet; then punched whatever he needed to punch and hit the air. He prayed, he said, all the way to the ground twelve minutes later; watched a million dollar plane blow up in a rice paddy while the base helicopter came to bring him home. This is the controlled use of the panic button.

Any precipitous, final action—action that lets you down—ought to be approached gingerly, definitely, deftly. People ought not run to divorce courts the first time they have an argument over the pay check. People ought not move from one town to another the first time they run into a difficult neighbor. People ought not hit the panic button precipitantly—but gingerly, deftly, definitely. The panic button of divorce, for example, ought never be used as a threat. The panic button of resignation ought never be used as a threat. The ultimate decision to sever relationships or try to break up an unbreakable thing like a home, ought not to be approached with haste. The panic button ought never be pushed out of revenge; it ought not be pushed in fright either. Panic buttons are mighty important pieces of equipment. Most life situations have a panic button, but you ought never push one to see if it works—especially if you are in the air! The ground check is another thing.

Most life problems have a panic button. There is an ultimate door, there is a last door; there is usually a parachute that will let you down in some sort of shape. But many a man has contacted the tower when he didn't have to jump. Even though there are legal ways of breaking up these relationships, even though there are doors and windows that lead to a certain kind of freedom, it is still true, and ought to be remembered, that people who approach the use of the panic button of divorce swiftly sometimes find that they left behind them all they ever had that was worth keeping. There are troubles, agonies, even despairs in married life, business life, and professional life; but the man who hopes to achieve some sort of peace and destiny never runs out too quickly. If he has to use a panic button, it is under control in sane, guided action. Most situations can be relieved if we cut out the elements of threat, haste, revenge, and panic. Many a man has contacted the tower who later did not jump.

POINT OF NO RETURN

ON A NAVY FLIGHT TO TRAVIS AIR FORCE BASE FROM TOKYO, ABOUT two o'clock in the morning the Navy commander passed my seat and noticed that I was awake. He invited me to the operations deck for a cup of coffee. As we chatted, I saw the navigator get up from his high stool, open a little window in the top of the plane, and sight an instrument at the stars through the overcast. He came back to his desk, made some calculations and I walked over to see his chart and his figures. I noticed that he had on a sheet of graph paper a projected line of flight from Hickam Air Force Base to Travis Air Force Base in California. There was an X marked where we were and then a couple of little red x's with the initials EP. I said to the navigator, "What does EP mean?" "Oh," he said, "you wouldn't understand it except in the language of the laymen—it is called *'point of no return'*." He said that this is a point beyond which we cannot turn back to Hickam Air Force Base; we have to go on to California. We were then an estimated five minutes from that point. "Then, there really is a point of no return?" And he said, "Yes,

85

practically, though we call it something else." Is there a point of no return in our lives?

There was for Miss Annie. She is just a little old lady living on the memory that once she had a chance to marry a man whose name now is known around the world. As a student in a little college town he fell in love with Miss Annie and they agreed to marry each other; but the girl's father said, "No, whoever came from that little old school and amounted to anything?" He wasn't going to have his daughter tied up with such a fellow. So out of obedience to her father Miss Annie didn't marry him. As a matter of fact, she didn't marry anybody; but for the last thirty years she has lived simply by virtue of the fact that once she could have married a real man. It was her point of no return. Somehow she never was able to recover her course and achieve anything like a full or useful life simply because frustration set in and she never could quite negotiate the course.

A rancher in West Texas explained the spotted life of success and failure he had lived. He didn't blame the drought, as most would, nor the cattle market, nor luck—he simply said, "You know my Daddy failed after my first year in college and I never did get to finish." As if that covered everything—that was his point of no return; he never quite recovered his course.

I have talked to people who explained everything that had ever come to them, good or bad, by saying, "Well, my marriage broke up, you know, when I was still quite young." I recall a man who said, "Well, my partner kicked out on me; I've never done well since." That was for him a point of no return. Through all the long years he has thrown everything that has ever needed explanation back to the fact that once when he was a very young man his partner failed him.

A man or a woman can blow up any disappointment that comes

to any dimension he or she wishes. But by this point of no return we simply mean that there is in such a person not enough drive or fuel to recover the course. He can't quite get back. Now it is granted that there are some places in the world to which a fellow would not wish to return. It is also to be granted that there are some conditions of mankind through which some have been to which we would not wish to return; but most of the time we are victims of an over evaluation of the handicaps. Many people live many, many years with an overvalued handicap. It is not as heavy as you make it. It is not as important as you have allowed it to be.

Where do you go to explain the trend your journey has taken? To what point when you were a youngster, or when you were older, do you go to mark out the place beyond which you just couldn't amount to very much? There are not many obstacles that leave you still alive past which a man cannot go—not many of them. There are one or two that a man can't pass but there aren't many. There aren't any connected with physical handicap or illness past which some friend of yours has not gone.

All over your city there are men who have handled every conceivable kind of obstacle and refused to permit it to be a point of no return. Must you sit your life through as one who could have married so and so but did not? Must you go your life through blaming something that happened in your childhood for your present inadequacies? There are not many calamities that leave you still alive past which a man cannot go.

III

THE HOPE WE HAVE

NOW WE ARE HERE

DURING THE WAR YEARS, WHEREVER YOU WERE, YOU DREAMED OF IT, you talked about it, you waited for it, you planned for it—and now it is here. In some backwoods camp job or pounding a typewriter in some CO's office or shoveling sulphur out of a ship's hold in the Merchant Marine or in a Sicilian hospital with encephalitis or on a desert tank or riding up to the break-through in Europe or hauling gas behind Patton's armies, "Someday," you said, "someday when I get out of this mess, I am going to have me a wife, and we are going to have us some kids, and we are going to have a home, and I am going to be in business." Or maybe you started along another tack. You said, "I am going to get me an education; I am going to have an office; I am going to have some nice furniture in it and it is going to look like somebody is working there. I am going to have my own practice, a wife, home, kids, and responsibility. I am going to go to P.T.A. and I am going to belong to the community. I am going to be a home man; I am going to achieve maturity. I am going to live well when life hits an even keel." And now you are here.

Now we are all here. All of us between thirty-two and forty-eight give or take a little, now we are here and the kids are growing up, and they have to have their teeth braced; and we are giving them all kinds of lessons to show them how to use their lanky legs. You have an equity in a house; or maybe you are ready to move to a better house. You had the best year you ever had last year, and you are looking for a better year this year. Your associations have been formed, you are working on community organizations, maybe you even go to church; you have been married just long enough now that the upholstery is beginning to fray. All in all things are doing well; they are not normal, you understand, but you decide they are better than normal ever was.

Away back there fifteen years ago, you thought, "My generation will be different." You said, "My generation will not forget this tragic business through which we have gone." You thought, "My generation of husbands and wives and families will remember this blood bath of agony and separation and we will not value the valueless; our day is going to be better than yesterday." Now it is fifteen years later—now you are here. And when you think back you are just a bit patronizing toward yourself about how crassly idealistic you were. You say, "I was a youngster then." And now you are jaded by the rushing demands of the first level of this race. You have come out on the first plateau and it is a much drier place than you thought it would be. It is not as nice, it is not as plush, and it is not as meaty, it is not as easy, and it is considerably duller. There is much more everyday everydayness in it; more dust, and you are considerably more rushed than you wish to be.

We are so involved in this "now we are here," that the tragic is gone, except in spots; although we get occasional scares here and there. Some good friend is called back in service and cracks up; or some comparatively young fellow dies suddenly with cancer he had had for months and didn't know about it; or some fellow two or three years younger than you are comes down with a vicious heart attack. But on the whole things are going along very well with you here, and you are inclined to forget all those great notions you had when you were there! The sand flats of Sicily, and North Africa, and the hedgerows, Dunkirk, or the Islands, are a long way behind you. And even though you lost nineteen hundred out of twenty-one hundred men on one little island you are able to live with it now, because it is so far behind you. On the whole you are almost wholly immersed in the material; almost wholly preoccupied with the requirements of filling your face, and putting something on your back, and taking care of your kids.

Now we are here! And if a man cannot belong where he is, he finds it difficult to belong anywhere. If a man, while he is here, has forgotten so much he once knew, he will find it difficult to learn again until some of life's personal burdens and tragedies come along to cut him down to size and peel him open to where he can feel the throbbing pulse of tragedy and pain and suffering and agony and need and joy and victory and conflict that is at the very center of life.

How can a man so harmless as a teacher, how can a man as dull as a minister, how can one so useless as a philosopher take us back into crisis? Whoever it is, whether it be an Unamuno or a Bertrand Russell, how can we go back into crisis so that we will remember what we once said from there that we would do and be when we got here? How can anyone show us that *now we are here?*

Here—where we said from there we would give anything on God's earth to be. Now we are here. And the fact that we are here means so little to us that we are almost wholly immersed in material desire, and in the desire to get from here to there.

Such a man misses life. It zips on by him. And the values that make life worth living anywhere slip away unnoticed through his occupation with the shallow, the valueless, and the humdrum, the repetitious, and the empty; the useless, the blinding, and the dulling effects of the everydayness of everyday materialisms.

How can we be reminded that now we are here? There are eternal potentials and values living in this moment, whoever we are and wherever we are we have no hope unless we can be reminded that a generation that will not live out its challenge in its here and now is not fit to live. We have no hope unless somehow we can be snatched into an awareness of our hereness; unless this hereness can become an involvedness. It is not enough to *be*, one must also be *here*. One becomes involved in the agonies and tensions and needs and despairs of his day. He no longer runs from them. He knows the emptiness of the various "escapes" from the situation as it is. But he comes to understand that any weakness and any strength and any glory and any failure has its meaning only in the hereness and the involvedness with which he gives himself to the true values and needs around him. Now we are here! But we shall not be able to stay here without a memory for the tragic that lies behind us to remind us to be very careful with our values. Nor shall we be able to go there without the realization that our hope begins in our being here where we are.

WHAT'S YOUR MISSION?

IN THE ENTRANCE TO OUR HEADQUARTERS BUILDING AT OSAN, KOREA, there is a huge sign which makes our business known. "The Mission of the 5th Air Force Advance is to maintain in Korea a joint operations center at the highest possible level of combat readiness, and to be prepared to conduct combat operations as directed." What is your mission?

At the close of the bitter years of the French Revolution someone asked Abbe Sieyes, "Father, what did you do during the Revolution?" With something of a twinkle in his eyes he said, "I survived." Sometimes that is a good work, just to survive. But is this all? If survival is the mission you have, it is not enough, for not many of us manage to survive long. We just can't arrange to be around as long as we would like.

Today the barber turned philosophical and began to talk about the changes he observed in the lives of people with whom he had grown up. Most of his friends had done reasonably well and are what would be called middle-class people. Now they have a little leisure on their hands, and sometimes at the end of the month they have a little money left over. Too many of them are bored with life and with living—drinking has become a problem, the dissolution of marriages goes on all around them; and, among some of the women with whom he has had friendship there is a dissolution of character. Perhaps this is a fair picture of a cross section of our times. Not many of us have a definite idea of who we are, what we are doing, and where we are going. I know people who just can't conceive of anyone ever giving himself to some cause. Their mission is to survive.

Now lots of us had the mission of survival back during the depression. I fell into conversation with a friend of mine in the Department of Public Safety about this. It turned out that we both had jobs digging ditches. We were fifteen hundred miles apart, it is true, but we were both digging ditches. I was impressed with a remark made by this responsible man, "I always tried to dig a beautiful ditch." Now if you have never dug ditches for a living you may not know that ditches can be dug so that they can have a certain symmetry and perfection and beauty of form. This leads me to speak of the dullness of the routine. As low and menial a task as we ordinarily think of ditch digging, it can really take on something of inspiration and beauty when a man tries to do it right. I know a woman whose job now is to stand at a counter and to insert a certain flavor of chocolate caramel in a corner of each box as it passes. If that young lady sees her job as a matter of dropping peppermint or caramel in the proper corner of a little box as it passes and never gets any other conception of life, or living, or mission, I would say she was in for a pretty drab time and the chances are she will be cross-eyed before she has worked six months.

A new understanding of mission is needed desperately. Now those who know any theology at all understand that by Christian work we have never meant just teaching a Sunday-school class. Work means the totality of all that a man produces. Work means all that comes as a result of my having lived. Work means everything that my personality produces anywhere it is at anytime. It ought to total up to good, somehow. I know some little and apparently very tired old ladies whose good that they have been, and are, and have produced, adds up to more than that of so-called philanthropists.

Do you have the kind of job in which you can see no value in the work—it's too drab? Whether you are packing candy or digging ditches the value is nearly always in the workers. You see, there is no work that really amounts to much that is not for *us*. That is to say, in the production of work and in its consumption, human personality is involved. That is the only reason Christian faith has anything to say to work and workers. It is because personality is involved. That is why Christianity has had through history such enduring power. It grasps the meaning of persons. And that is why I get so exercised about what is happening to minority groups of personality among us. The Christian view of life has no right whatsoever to ever consider itself above the value of all others. Christian personality sees in each one who lives a universe of potential. It sees a tremendous spiritual power in each man on its way to happening.

I was tired of looking out over the Yellow Sea toward Red China; getting up cold, sleeping in tents; working my head off, I was homesick. But one day, walking around a rice paddie with some men on their way to work, I began to ask myself, "What am I really doing here?" And a better sense of mission came to me. "Maybe I had come to say that no man had to go home less than he came out." A boy wrote me once to say, "Thank you for coming. I have less than when I came over here, and I have some scars, but I don't aim to go back less than I am now."

I don't know what your plans are, but you will wind up less than you are now unless you have a mission that somehow involves personality and what you can mean to the persons around you. What is your mission?

What did you do this year? "Oh, I survived." It is not enough. None of us can survive very long. What is your mission at your work? It ought to involve the totality of all that you are, all that you make, all that adds up to life that comes from you in terms of personality that exists, that lives, that grows or dies, that hurts, that needs around you. There isn't any other way to define Christian work except in terms of the workers. Anywhere a man does an honorable job where people are present he is eligible to have a mission. What is your mission?

THE LEAP OF FAITH

Most everyone you meet is looking for a sure thing. Life would be great if all the element of risk could be removed. Whether this concerns the outcome of a horse race or a prize fight doesn't really matter. What the bettor wants is a sure thing; the knowledge that what he risks will not be lost. The same thing would be nice for investment or insurance. And wouldn't it be nice if someone could write a marriage contract in which there would be no element of risk whatsoever? Wouldn't it be wonderful if a man could get a guarantee of that sort on any kind of real-estate deal? Everybody is looking for a sure thing. This was the appeal of those fabulous giveaway radio and TV shows. Nothing is risk, and anything is gain—whether it be a carton of cigarettes or $64,000. Guaranteed returns! What a powerful phrase that has been in advertising. All of us want a sure thing.

This is particularly true with respect to the big gamble—life itself. With all our hearts we want every element of risk removed that can be removed. And this, strangely enough, is the weakness of those timid men of knowledge who will not go for faith because faith is not, and never can be, a matter of knowledge. Whether they speak in language like this or not, at the bottom of the refusal of every man to commit himself to faith is the realization that really there is too much risk in faith. Therefore, we cannot live by faith. The risk is too great.

In the last twenty years a strange thing has been happening to our vaunted knowledge and our ways of knowing. Those few in the world who think a little have come to realize how little of their knowledge is knowledge and how much of it is conjecture, assumption, or reliance on laws that are still subject to question. In other words, we have become aware of the "relativity of most of our knowledge." Because we cannot be certain of our knowledge we stand on the lip of an abyss of meaninglessness. In order to confront it, in order to explain the new physics, men have had to invent new algebras that I can't even spell. They have come out with geometries that leave poor Euclid in the limbo of oblivion. New kinds of mathematics have become necessary to explain the new physics. And this has a devastating effect on the calm reliance we have had so long for our old knowledge. Suddenly it began to be clear that faith is what we have been operating on all the time, for our knowledge is devastatingly partial. To our amazement, after hundreds of years of brilliant scientific enterprise, we are made aware that our "knowledge" is painfully inexact; and that the main thing we still have to go on is faith.

That mighty man, perhaps the mightiest man of our time, Albert Einstein, was operating on the basis of a mighty faith. At least I begin to get that notion when the brilliant Alfred North Whitehead calls the demonstration of Einstein's idea of bending light rays a project of "the spirit." Maybe I have to draw my conclusions about everything on the basis of insufficient evidence. Maybe the only way reality ever becomes something human life can know and taste for the moment is on the basis of insufficient evidence. Maybe the only way marital fidelity ever becomes fact is that two people have drawn conclusions about each other's love on the basis of insufficient evidence. Maybe old Samuel Butler, dead these decades, was right when he said, "Life is the art of drawing sufficient conclusions on the basis of insufficient evidence." This is the point all men of faith must come to sooner or later. And this is the point where a new beginning becomes possible for any man of knowledge, of doubt, of agnosticism, or of atheism if he will see the perilous partialness of all his knowledge, if he will become aware that every venture upon which his spirit has ever thrust itself, every human involvement and every personal commitment has been involvement and commitment made on the basis of insufficient evidence. And the difference is made up, whether he likes the word or not, out of faith.

Some months ago there came to me the hand-written words of a friend, "Life is always at some turning point." That is to say, there are no straight lines in life. It is a tremendous sentence if you live with it a little while. Life is always at some turning point. Now the difference in whether that life is turning around a circle, or in a section of an ellipse, or whether it is going off in a meaningless series of vagaries has to do with what that life turns around. Certainly those who live at all know that life is always turning in one direction or another. Heraclitus showed us centuries before Christ that life is involved with change and flux. But around what is life turning?

The great Martin Heidegger comes out at the end saying something like this: "The gods are silent; we wait for whatever god there is to speak." That is one place a man can come out. Or another comes out like Homer Smith in *Man and His Gods* to say, "There is no god to speak; we are alone in a world that gets its only meaning from what we can put into it." Or there is another answer.

The men who realize the dread partialness of our knowledge, that all of life's conclusions are drawn on the basis of insufficient evidence, and that the venture of faith cuts into all of life's thrusts and explorations, perhaps such men of maturity will be willing to listen for the moment at least to the rustle of the testimony of the heart of the race with all its symbolic yearnings, and symbolic meanings, and, if you please, symbolic answers.

Man always makes a leap—it's a leap of despair, or it's a leap of faith. There is infinite risk in either. There is infinite risk in making a leap off into meaninglessness from knowledge that can end in despair. There is also an infinite risk in making the leap of faith that can end only in a moral obligation. But there is a difference between despair and faith. Men who have made a leap of faith are men whose lives are marked with conscience, moral order, integrity, and a sense of destiny.

All of us must make conclusive commitments on the basis of inconclusive evidence; and everything we "know" rests on the basis of inconclusive testimony. The leap of faith is the only hope this race has ever found for bringing itself beyond what it is in the direction of what it can become.

CARVE YOUR OWN DIGNITY

ON DAYS LIKE TODAY THINGS THAT I CANNOT GET DONE KEEP STANDING around and shouting at me. Usually, here, my mind turns to Señor Mura.

A few miles out of the city of Asuncion, Paraguay, the Chacos (Brush) begins to change into Matto Grosse (Big Jungle). I rode one day in a truck some sixty miles on clay road, the last ten miles through mud, to come at last to a jungle hacienda. There was a pile of fire wood thirty or forty feet high at the gate, and on top of it the welcome commitee—five little boys and a couple of goats— were enjoying the sun as its rays reached between the limbs of great trees around them. With a blanket thrown over his shoulders, for it was chilly even in midmorn, and with his large gnarled feet split by sandal thongs, with those huge, misshapened hands extended, a very fine looking, very old, very steady kind of little

101

man, Señor Mura, came out from under a shaded patio to bid us welcome to his house.

We sat on great mahogany benches and talked an hour, then it was time for lunch. It was a feast that beggars description: little slices of beef dipped in a kind of meal and fried very crisp; sausages, and mutton; a dozen exotic dishes, vegetables, and the plantain that grows on trees; wonderful fruit. Then it was time for a little walk before siesta. We walked through his banana groves and his pineapple ranges; we saw his cattle, watering pools, and cotton.

After an hour or so of sleep the old man sent for me and I came into a clay-floored room with tile walls, a simple picture, a bed made of cords stretched across mahogany logs, a single pad folded across the cords. It was a Spartan room; one chair, one bed, one picture, one pitcher, one glass, and two or three books. As we talked there unfolded a remarkable tale in almost perfect English as a tiny, very old, Italian saint told me how he had "carved his dignity" out of the jungle.

Some sixty years before in Los Angeles, he had learned to speak English. He had worked as a laborer on the Panama Canal; during those years there came upon him a desire to amount to something and he immigrated from the Canal Zone to Paraguay. With his own huge hands he had carved his dignity out of a jungle. He married a Paraguayan girl, and twelve children had been born into that home. Now he was thronged with fine grandchildren. The sons were working the plantation, except for three or four who had moved off into the city of Asuncion. After the death of his wife he was coming at last to a mature old age crowned with serenity and dignity. As we talked through the hours of that long afternoon, I became aware of many heart-breaking things—discouragements, revolutions, war—and yet always I was aware of this central core of tremendous dignity; and I was conscious that I was in the presence of a very great man.

Along toward the shank of the afternoon, he began to raise questions in the field of church history. I was dumbfounded at such historical literacy in an Italian immigrant who had gone from Italy to California to the Canal Zone to Paraguay to carve out his own life in the middle of a jungle amid his Moravian neighbors and the hundred thousand or so white Russians who had worked their way across from China after the Boxer Rebellion. Here was this farmer asking technical questions about groups like the Petrobrusians, the Albigensian, the Waldensians, and other early Protestant groups. I was even more impressed that here a thousand miles from "anywhere" was a tiny tremendous man who in technical knowledge, in native dignity, had contributed to life, had taken from life, had found a kingdom, and had become a king. It came to me that I must carve my dignity out of a jungle also.

We are not going to achieve our dignity as men by settling great stretches of land that are already settled, or by raising bananas, they don't do too well here; and pineapples are not for this climate or this soil. But modern living, we all confess, is a maze of jungle-like growth, it is truly Matto Grosse. And this maze of jungle growth in modern living constitutes a major threat to selfhood. And therefore selfhood is a task to be achieved. What I admired in my friend Mura was not so much just his dignity, but with him selfhood was already an accomplished task. He had carved his dignity, I say, out of a jungle.

There are several aspects of this true selfhood, this dignity for which we were born. It may be in the jungle of one of these office buildings, it may be in the maze of the school system, it could be anywhere men have to meet the problems of everyday life. Selfhood is not given, it is a task to be achieved. It begins in the de-

103

velopment of our ability to recognize value. We exercise the power of choice that is native to us, and pick the valuable. But in picking the valuable, we must commit ourselves to the acceptance of responsibility; and in this acceptance of responsibility for the life around us and for our contribution to the life around us, we have to acquire the capacity for waiting. We can't have what we wish before payday. We can't even have what we wish when payday comes, and therefore this capacity for waiting demonstrates the limitations of our own physical power. We learn in the light of what we choose to value, in what we accept responsibility for, to commit ourselves to the tension that lives between the two in a way that carves out this selfhood from the jungle.

I once asked the chief of the Texas Rangers why he employed a certain fellow. The Colonel had found this lad years before on a pipeline job with a gang of laborers down on the Rio Grande. "I went into the shack where he was living and it was paneled, trimmed, and swept; it was so clean and spotless that any woman could have been welcomed there; and it was an indication that here was a man who would be more than he was in any set of circumstances." Perhaps even on a pipeline job, perhaps even in a freshmen mathematics class, perhaps even in checking groceries behind a counter a man is responsible for carving out his own dignity from a jungle. Everything opposes, everything in our time will sap your selfhood, but it is your responsibility to carve your own dignity out of the jungle that surrounds you.

THE DISFRANCHISED

ON THE FRINGES OF ALL PROFESSIONS, ON THE SIDE-SEATS OF THE churches, on the edges of the Christian ministry, there lives a host of men and women in our time, in our town, whom we would call disfranchised. They are not truly accepted for participation in some church or in some other institution because the creed of the particular institution won out and is more valuable than personality. Some particular rule or set of rules won out over the value that was posited in the person. This is what institutions are all about. Institutions are designed not to tolerate much difference. Institutional life is safe life, it is a buttressed life, it is bulwarked by opinions and rules and creeds and forms. And here in America, and everywhere else, all through history, there have been men and women who simply cannot fit. Much of the time they cannot fit because they recognize the limits of the institutional. They sometimes sense within themselves that our institutional churches, our institutions of government, our institutions of life, even of education, just somehow will not in every instance get the job done. Such people offer a mighty hope to us.

This I believe to be the point of one of the most perfect short stories in literature—it is a story Jesus told. Perhaps you would like to name an institutional frame in today's world in which Jesus Christ would be entirely at home. I have no candidates to offer. But he did tell the perfect short story—he said, "A certain man was going down from Jerusalem to Jericho; and he fell among robbers who stripped him and beat him and departed, leaving him half dead. And by chance a certain priest was going down that way: and when he saw him, he passed by on the other side. And in like manner a Levite also, when he came to the place, and saw him, passed by on the other side." And then, adding insult to injury, the Master went ahead to say that a certain Samaritan

105

on his way from Jerusalem to Jericho came upon him, picked him up, bound his wounds, soaked them in oil, put him on his own beast, brought him to an inn, paid his fare, left money for his period of convalescence, and said if there should be more, he would pay it when he came back through.

One of the points of the story is the frequency with which the institutional, represented by the priest and the Levite—those organized to do good—may miss true need. And the fundamental point of the story is the demand for the neighbor. The hero of the story is a disfranchised man from whom nothing is expected. The society, the structures of his day have rejected him. No one ever expected anything high or fine or noble from a Samaritan.

In the last ten years I have seen more than two thousand pages of tortuously written manuscript done by at least a score of people, much of it written late at night. They all have this in common— they have felt themselves disfranchised by society, and have poured out their own thoughts to themselves, usually for no eyes but their own, late into the night. Among these who frequently write this way, I have a very special favorite. He usually comes to see me about every three years. He has soft blue eyes, a very easy kind voice, a mild manner, and he writes like Sören Kierkegaard. He is disfranchised: he is truly Christian.

Once upon a time he expected to be a minister, and was in a Christian church, but he just couldn't fit. There were elements of freedom and inspiration in his personality, and this meant that no code or creed or rule, or set of dogmas could quite confine him. He just couldn't fit. So it was that in due process, according to his own framework where he then served, he was disfranchised. On his last visit I asked, "What do you do now to exercise your calling since you have no congregation and no pulpit?" He answered, *"Who says I have no congregation? There is a lot of grief and pain that I can sit by."*

In every block I know, there is the demand for the neighbor, and for any man or woman, there is "a lot of grief and pain that a fellow can sit by." Regardless of your institutional status, regardless of whether or not you participate in a certain pattern or framework, regardless of your acceptance or denial of institutionally ensconced values and value judgments, all over your city, there is a lot of grief and pain that a fellow can sit by.

Let me salute my neighbor, he knows who he is. I salute him for his restoration to a larger franchise—the franchise of the kingdom of God.

ANONYMOUS PRIESTS

TOWNS TAKE THINGS FOR GRANTED. NEIGHBORHOODS HAVE A WAY, ALL institutions have a way of taking things for granted. If a job is well and regularly done, a man can spend his life doing it, and the city never needs to know his name. Consequently all cities fail to see their less spectacular ministrants of mercy. We fail to know our anonymous priests by name.

This is why you never know your mailman's name—do you? And, if you did not pay your yardman by check, you wouldn't know his name at all. You would call him "Joe" or whatever name you've heard. This is why you don't even know your service-station man's faith, or whether he has children or not. And your meter reader you wouldn't know if you saw him. The only connection you have with your garbage man is to howl if he doesn't show up.

This is an ungodly sort of situation when I don't need to know a man's name. Sometimes there comes a man who refuses to let his job keep him anonymous. He refuses to let his job confine him and keep me from needing to know his name. Here and there comes a man whose way of doing his work is such that I have to find out who he is. That is to say his job becomes his way of giving himself to God. He becomes a nameless priest engaged in a ministry of mercy. And such a man may bless a city from a corner, or from a fruit stand, or in a hundred different places, so that I go up and ask his name.

A man like this, bigger than some, is Charlie Gonzales. If you have been a patient at Holy Cross, or at Seton, or at Brackenridge, or at St. David's, you know Charlie Gonzales. You know him as faithful and regular and courteous and considerate. The first day you are able to read (now I don't know how Charlie knows this) there Charlie is. And on the second day, if you happen to be asleep when he comes by, he leaves the paper and will collect for it later. If you have thought of him at all you have thought of him as that special newspaperman at the hospital. But he is more. He is just a whole lot more than this.

On his regular rounds at St. David's last week Charlie came to a sick man's door and said, "Would you like to have a paper?" "No!" the patient answered, "I don't need a paper. I need someone to pray for me." And Charlie said, "I can do that too!" He dropped his papers, went to his knees, and prayed. Edith Coleman, the supervisor, overheard this and told me about the great calm that descended on a troubled man. She said it was as if Charlie were a priest! "I can do that, too," Charlie said.

No customer of his had ever known it, but *Charlie had been praying at every door for twenty years or more!*

It isn't enough to do your job faithfully and well. There is an overage; there is an overplus, through which a man at any kind of job becomes one who assumes the responsibility for the moral and spiritual welfare of those he passes. That is to say, any kind of work can become an avenue through which a man offers himself to a wider, deeper, human need than the mere fulfillment that his job requires. There is a sense in which any honest work becomes a channel through which God's help can come into the lives of those who are touched in this work. This is a daily sacrament.

You have no right to serve in whatever job you have so that people never need to know your name. A newsman delivering daily papers can get such a concept of his daily work that he becomes chaplain—a priest of God—who intercedes for the welfare of those he passes. The rooms into which he goes become a kind of cathedral, and the thing he delivers becomes an instrument of blessing. Whoever would have thought there could be a healing way of delivering newspapers?

There is a healing way of doing a job. There are anonymous priests in every town who without benefit of clergy, professional training, or theology become a means of healing, a way of blessing: a beatitude, a beneficence, a hope, a help. It happens on any day's journey, anywhere you meet an anonymous priest.

WHO ARE THE BARBARIANS?

"ANY TWELVE-YEAR-OLD BOY IS A BARBARIAN," I SAID, IN ANSWER TO her question. But the look on her face let me know she was quite serious so I tried to give her a better answer: " 'barbarian' comes from a word the Greeks used to describe the people whose language was a 'bar-bar' sound that meant nothing to civilized people. Barbarians are any wild, unrefined people not at home in civilized work, in a civilized world." But now I am taking my answer back because I was dead wrong.

It all depends on who answers the question. If you had asked the Greeks about this they would have said "the barbarians are those wild people who live just north of us in Macedonia." But it was out of Macedonia that King Philip came to rule the Greeks. And the son of this barbarian king was the fabulous Alexander the Great.

If you had asked the Romans, they would have said "the barbarians are those long-bearded fellows north of us, those axemen across the Rhine. They are those crazy fighting fools who will stay fourteen years in the field with an army without even going home. They are those fellows who wear the horns of animals and skins of beasts, and fight with axes and spears and clubs." Some Romans would have said, "They are the finest fighters we have ever met." One Roman general was proudly named Germanicus as a tribute to the barbarians. One barbarian, Maximus Thrax, weighed approximately four hundred pounds, could eat fourteen pounds of meat at a meal, wore a woman's bracelet as a ring on his finger, and was actually emperor of the Romans for a while. But along about A.D. 410 one of those people they called "barbarian" pushed his spear up the nose of Terminus, the god of the never-receding Roman boundary, and tipped him over in the dust—

forever. On his heels, those wildbearded fellows from the North began to be kings in the city of Rome.

Who are the barbarians? Well, the answer depends upon who answers the question. To Charlemagne, the Huns and the Magyars were the barbarians. The Germans call the Poles barbarians. In eighth-century Spain, they said the Moslems who had brought so much culture to us were barbarians. Or if you had asked in ancient China, they would have said, "the Mongols and the Khans who have come to rule us." Actually, the barbarians are those we have not conquered who will one day rule us!

Ask a modern European (or an American), "Who are the barbarians?" The answer is likely to be "the Russians." But for centuries now, Russia has been claiming to be the "third Rome." It was more than a thousand years ago that gold plate went on the vaulted arches and domes of the great cathedrals in the city of Moscow. "After Rome and Constantinople comes Moscow!" Throughout the literature of the Russian people you find this wild Slavic, Russian faith that the messianic people sent by God are the Russian people, and that they are destined to rule the world.

Ask Russia, "Who are the barbarians?" "The Franks, the people of the West, the Americans, these are the barbarians!"

In today's world, my answer and these answers are far wrong. With colonialism dead and done for, with the remaining elements of the British Empire breaking up, to ask "Who are the barbarians?" is not to ask for a local answer. The barbarians are everywhere!

Who are the barbarians? If you will read history with any sort of discernment at all, if you can look past the wild skins and pagan drums and crude implements, can feel past the crude beginnings of language and literature, you can begin to understand that there is a very real sense in which *the barbarian is the one who is teachable enough to take on new ideas.* He has not come along so far in the world that he shuts all his senses to the taking on of ideas that can come to him from some other culture, from some other clime, or from some other faith. He is a man who is teachable enough that *he can endure a new idea!*

Barbarians are men who are far enough from home, far enough out on a venture, that they have to stick with the tribe. They are men cut off because they are a long way from where they are headed, and *they have to belong to one another.*

Barbarians are those who are rugged enough that *they can stand the punishment of adjustment to crisis.* This is a peculiar kind of ruggedness required at any time of cultural upheaval and change. Those who survive are those whose spirits stand the punishment of adjustment, and these are almost never the patrician peoples of a culture. The stamina moves to the fringes.

Finally, the barbarians, everywhere you can see them for what they truly are, are those people who are needy enough that *they will respond to help from outside themselves.* They are those who have themselves so little that they can afford to be generous.

I've changed my mind about the barbarians. I hope we are barbarians. I hope we are teachable enough to be able to recover some ideas that we dropped long ago. I hope we are barbarian enough, far enough from where we are headed, to be forced to stick together for the sake of the mission upon which we are headed. I hope our spirits are rugged enough to stand the punishment of adjustment; that we are needy enough to respond to help from beyond ourselves; that we know we have so little that we can afford to be generous with what we have got.

The barbarians are everywhere. There isn't any race, or any section in the world which has a corner now on this kind of spiritual barbarism. I hope there is left in us enough of the rugged, the needy, the homesick, that we can face this crisis of adjustment with help from whatever source it can come to an openhearted and generous minded people.

Who are the barbarians? It depends on who answers the question.

THE HIGH CALLING

DURING LIMA'S CELEBRATION OF THE FOUR HUNDREDTH ANNIVERSARY of the founding of the University of San Marcos, I went to the cathedral to see the body of Pizzaro. This frail remnant of a man with an ax hole in his chest was now a brown skeleton of broken bone structure and armor: all that remained of Pizzaro. As I stood involved in an old sixteenth-century tragedy, a thin Peruvian in the brown robe, rope belt, and sandals of a Dominican lay brother approached and interrupted in good English my fascination with Pizarro. A teacher of archaeology at San Marcos, he had spotted me as *"Norte Americano"* and we began a brief encounter.

I remember his eyes—brown pools of concerned vitality—I remember the largeness and beauty of his eyes in his frail little body; but most of all I remember a passionate interest in the United States of America. He had passionate concern to know what was truly our spirit and question after question he fired at me. Presently, as I turned to go, he nailed me with this: "Those of us who think most deeply here in Peru believe that our God has given peculiar blessings to your nation; we think she is a land of destiny and high calling. *We only wish that her exports matched her calling.*"

This has been something that I have been totally unable to forget—an aged Dominican professor, in a very ancient university, in a very old land, telling a young American Protestant whom he had never seen before and would never see again, that his nation's exports ought to match her high calling!

I remembered what I had seen on the shopping streets between the churches and the public buildings of Lima that day: the artifacts of our "coca-cola culture"; I remembered the cheap jewelry; the trinkets of trade with "backward people"; I remembered the cheap pictures and the pornographic literature "printed in U.S.A." in Spanish. I looked at the people and thought what they could have received, and the Dominian brother's words forced their way deep inside me. There, for a moment, I felt as though I was responsible for the sin of the whole nation.

You see, nations as nations have obligation, because nations as nations develop personal entity. Nations as nations have a spirit; nations as nations have a center of value. And there was in Lima a mighty contradiction between our high calling and our limited awareness of this call! It was as if he had said, "If you really knew your calling your exports would reflect your knowledge of that calling." I thought of the hunger for steel plows and tractors and technical know-how; the need for verve, and energy and dash; and the courage needed to make the mistakes that are necessary to progress. I thought of what we might be giving and receiving, if our exports were right, in such an old and wonderful land as Peru. What must happen to us before our exports can match our high calling, our opportunity, our obligation, our responsibility? Then I was drawn up sharply in awareness that each man I know has a calling, the same calling, and this is the Christian ethic.

This high calling is that everything that proceeds from a man shall be done in the sight of and to the glory of God. Put in a more acceptable way for some of my friends who would not accept a Christian frame of reference this means that everything that issues from the lone man, just like everything exported by the mighty nation, is a reflection of his sense of his own potential. It means that everything that issues from a man is this man's work. It is a part of himself, and it reflects, it expresses his impression of his own potential. Every man, in or out of the Christian faith, is called to let that that comes out of him be a reflection of his high calling. The New Testament has a "high view" of man. It thinks that man can become fit for fellowship with God; but not unless the work that comes out of him, everything that issues from him—his home, his friends, his family, his work, his love, is an expression of this high calling to become. We live on a level lower than we have been called to live.

I can't forget my little Dominican. He is with me every day. He reminds me that my exports ought to match my calling; and that this is a hope we have.

ACCEPTING THE ADVERSE

"See that little Japanese fellow there with his mop?" the doctor said. "He used to be a major in the Japanese Imperial Army. He had reverses, to put it mildly." But he knows how to live with them, and now pushes a mop down a corridor in an American hospital near Tokyo.

I asked a warrant officer why a particular waitress was treated with such politeness by the airmen in his mess. "Oh," he said, "they know Mamma-San's story—you see, she was once a wealthy lady and her husband was one of the famous aces, a colonel of the Japanese Air Force, but he died on Fujiyama and her property was in Hiroshima." She waits tables in a sergeants' mess on an American Air Base, accepting her reverses.

Here in my town there lives a colonel of the U.S. Army who was shot through both armpits when the Chinese troops crossed the Yalu at daylight one morning. He commanded his forces from a litter on a tank tread for six hours until the Eighth Army broke through to relieve him. And now, totally paralyzed from his armpits down, he has had to keep demonstrating the acceptance of the adverse.

There are great demands for the accepting of the adverse in other ways: Joseph Klausner lists those with moral courage enough to overcome the great handicap of epilepsy. In the field of religion, he cites Augustine, Mohammed, Bernard of Clairvaux, Savonarola, Jakob Boehme and Swedenborg. In the field of politics, he cites Julius Caesar, Peter the Great, and Napoleon I. In the field of letters he cites Pascal, Rousseau, and Dostoevski. How does it happen that men can overcome things like epilepsy, rifle balls through armpits, lost stations and careers? We call the acceptance of these unanswerable situations moral courage. But what makes it possible for people to overcome unovercomables?

All of us come at sometime to the edge of things. Here we are met by *a sense of the inescapable*. Way down deep we know that major tragedies are inescapable. It is the minor ones that call forth the loudest outcry. In the presence of the inescapable we settle down. I remember a little girl on the banks of the Han River with the utmost grief in her eyes and tears on her face—she was literally aghast in the face of the great tragedy that had happened to her.

The family's wash pan was floating off down the Han River! A Korean boy on the main bridge into Seoul spilled his school books and then wrecked his bicycle trying to get to those books before a truck ran over them—tears were literally streaming down his face. The same youngsters watched impassively a moment later when a truck ran down an old man. In the big things that flood over us as an accomplished fact—we settle down. It is the little things that upset us. A doctor told me he had never seen an hysterical man die. In the face of the inevitable, in the face of the edge of things, men have a tendency to settle down. It is our sense of the inescapable thing, and is an element in moral courage.

There also is required, in accepting our reverses, a *new evaluation of the remnant*. A man learns to take better care of the treasure that is left. A new evaluation is put on family. Possessions that remain become more precious. The routines that are still open to him, or the opportunities that may still await him become immeasurably important. A new evaluation of what we have left is essential in overcoming the unovercomable.

Moral courage demands a *belief in the possibility of improvement*. This is the confident expectation that things will not always be as they are now. We have a hope that things will improve.

And finally, there is *the sense of communion* that will not let us quit. By this I mean that we are aware that we are caught in a fellowship of people who share our agonies, our difficulties, our weaknesses, our losses—that whatever our particular moral or personal or physical or spiritual situation in this life, there are many who are in the same boat.

These qualities are the functional makeup of what we call the "power of accommodation," and this is moral courage. In *The Way of All Flesh* Samuel Butler says, "A life will be successful or not according as the power of accommodation is equal or unequal to the strain of adjusting to the internal and external changes." In us, that power of accommodation appears as moral courage. Courageous action in the face of things we cannot change is the result. Our ability to adjust, the power of accommodation, is the means, it is the way we get it done.

That sense of the inescapable which gives us a holy calm when we are face to face with the inevitable, what is it but a sense of destiny to be accepted? That new evaluation of what we have left is a definition of the processes of *faith*. That belief in the possibility that something else good can still come, what is that but *hope?* And the sense of communion, a sense of others being caught in these situations with us, is this not really the *fellowship of the saints?*

Destiny, faith, hope, and the communion of the saints. In these a man rises to meet the demands when life tumbles in. Here moral courage comes to him.

In a town I used to know very well an old friend has just learned that that pain he has had in his hip for a year or two is not rheumatism or arthritis, or sciatica; it is cancer, and he hasn't very long to live. I have known Mr. Jim since I was just a boy; I would expect him to do as he is doing. He is selling his land, his feed stores, his cattle. He is settling all his accounts and getting everything in shape. He is resigning his posts and committees at the church. He is preparing his loved ones for this inevitable thing. But in the meantime, he is up and down the main street. He will have a new joke for you most of the mornings, and likely you will be able to hear him laugh around the corner. He knows that destiny, and hope, and faith, and the communion of the saints will add up to give a man courage when it is needed.

YEARS OF THE LOCUST

"THE BITTEREST SORROW THAT A MAN CAN KNOW," SAYS HERODOTUS, "is to wish very much to do something and not to be able to do it." There is a sorrow more bitter than this: to wish very much to do something and to do it, and then to find that it was not worth the doing; this is bitter indeed.

These are the years of the locust; the years that you worked for nothing; the years that your dream thinking sapped your opportunity; the years that you thought you could make it alone; the years when you had no vision; the times when you thought all opinions opposite to your own were stupid; those tragic years when your own youngsters, or your own wife, or your own husband, or your own parents had the capacity to wrench your heart out and did. All of us have times in our lives that seem to be sheer waste.

In the Book of Joel you can see falling to shreds the strength, purpose, and destiny of a mighty empire. These are years of the locust, too, but it meant nothing to me until I saw the memoirs of an old friend from South Africa. G. J. Rousseau, telling of his Dutch boyhood in South Africa, describes the locust swarm. Billions of insects six or seven inches long swarm and settle on the crops. In flight they block out the sun and descend in piles of living insects that destroy everything in sight. The years the locusts come they get everything. There is not a blade of grass; there is not a green leaf left in the country where the swarms of locusts settle. The natives round up the horses and cattle in the country and drive them, screaming and yelling and pounding, across acres of locusts trying to pound their bodies into the soil before they have a chance to leave their eggs. At the end of their short life's span, these locusts pile up in windrows and die by the millions. But on the years that locusts come, nothing is left for a farmer, nothing is left for a grower, nothing is left on a plantation or ranch. The years the locusts come nothing remains that is edible. These are "the years the locust hath eaten."

These are the years that you worked and some locust got everything. These were years you were not able to focus on who you really are, and what you really are to be and to do. These were the years when you worked for the wrong end of things, when your values were wrong, when your direction was wrong, when your heart power was focused on values that were of no true concern. These were the years of your arrogance when you thought you could make it alone. These years of your pride were years that the locusts got. These were the years when you had no vision, when you had no desire beyond yourself; these were the years when life revolved around you and you had not yet resigned the center of the universe. These were the years when you had not learned the true meaning of ignorance. Or worse still, these were the years when your own youngsters could bring a swarm of locusts that destroyed everything in your heart.

In this strange little book of Joel an unheard of thing is promised: *"I will restore to you,"* and this is amazing language, *"I will restore to you the years which the swarming locust has eaten."* Is there any place on earth or off the earth where these lost years can be restored? I think not. Surely the writer of the Book of Joel is spouting poetry when he uses this kind of language.

Yet, says Rousseau, the greatest crops that the South African farmer ever reaps are those crops that grow up through the land that has been fertilized by the corpses of last year's locusts!

This is what the poet is talking about in the Book of Joel. He is saying that the lost years are not lost years at all but become a fertilizing influence to make the crown of life what it could never have been without the years you thought you had lost. If a man is aware of the years the locusts have destroyed; if he can reach a true judgment about his source and his strength, he can allow the dead years he thought he had lost to become useful. The capacity of judgment that comes to a man *after* his locust years is of unbelievable richness. He knows a thousand ways *not* to do— this is part of the fertilizing power of the years the locusts destroyed. He ought to know a hundred contrasts that will not work. He ought to know a score of ways to see what has been negative converted to something positive. The corpses of his own dead locusts feed the new crops he can raise.

The ancient cry of Joel, used so grandly by Mendelssohn in his *Elijah,* "Rend your hearts and not your garments," means here, "quit tearing your shirts over things that are inevitable, reach an inner decision about your sources of strength and the moral demands that life puts upon you; then absorb, and use, and grow, through the fertilizing power of the years that were wholly negative, the times you thought 'the locusts had eaten.'" There is a hope of restoration for what the locusts have eaten, if you believe in the fertilizing power of the years you have lost.

THE NIGHT SHIFT

My friend at the next table remarked to me that life had gotten so messy for her that she was going to have to take a "ten-minute think." But, she prophesied, if she ever did, she would wind up more confused than ever, because everything seemed so "temporary"! At Duke University, A. C. Reid said it in different words: "Whatever man earns nature eventually collects." The same truth appears in the seventeenth-century Quaker who said there would come a time when all our "gathered-in things" and all our "taken-on things" would fail us. Evelyn Underhill claimed that every man in the Christian life sooner or later goes on *the night shift.*

I think the figure needs no real amplification. When a man goes on the night shift it is obvious that his whole system of living changes. His schedules change, his habits change; his attitudes change; his desires change because what he calls valuable changes. There comes a time in most men's lives, I say, when everything "gathered in" and everything "taken on" pales to absolute insignificance alongside the central problem of health, or destiny, or the answer to the question about who he is. Any man can tell when he is on the night shift. Evelyn Underhill is right; all men must sometime go on the night shift.

Whole families frequently go on the night shift together. They live through long, dark nights of the soul, long twisting valleys— sometimes filled with pain, and frequently filled with pointless suffering. And what is sometimes worse, they are filled with a dread anxiety that cannot be settled one way or another. But regardless of how long, or how frequently you have been on night shift it has its own compensations.

During school vacations I frequently found myself working the night shift where my father was the supervisor. It had its compensations. There were roaring fires in furnaces; there was the hustle and bustle, the light of hot steel against the black darkness of the coke stacks in the night outside the plant. There were the fabulous midnight suppers that Mother fixed for Daddy and me. Along with the hustle and bustle, and light, and roar, and the midnight supper and the friends and the association—there are compensations on the night shift. I can trace some awfully important scales of value to the fact that I was once, for a period of time, responsible for living the night shift.

The biggest compensation that comes to a man living on the night shift is the anticipation of dawn. Have you noticed, when you have driven all night, how bad the hours are from one o'clock past three, past half-past four? In the summer months along about a quarter of five the first gray streaks of the new day begin to light up the sky ahead of you if you are headed east; or you find yourself glancing furtively over your shoulder, if you are driving west, to catch the earliest foregleams of the coming dawn. You know that a night drive, or a night shift, or a long valley, or a high climb cannot last forever. We get comfort in these night shifts of ours by the realization that there are processes in life.

The prophet Isaiah caught it in the question from the darkness, "What of the night?" The answer came back: The day comes. But don't take too much comfort in the coming of the day, because the night will come again too. Our comfort comes from the realization that we do live in a process that cannot leave us on these night shifts forever.

There is demanded a certain kind of character for night-shift living. Indeed, in night-shift living this character comes to its richest and fullest expression. Fundamentally, the kind of character demanded for night-shift living is the gift of Christian faith. An acquaintance of mine was recently subjected to tremendous tension through the death of his wife. He reported later that a minister came but he just read something from a book! The character for night-shift living is best demonstrated in the book the Christians call the Holy Scriptures. Night-shift living is the reason many of those characters got in that big book. David's terrific grief over Absalom when, he cries, "O Absalom, my son, my son!"

123

is fundamentally no different from the agony of the soul of Christ himself in Gethsemane as he cries, "O Jerusalem, Jerusalem . . . how often would I have gathered thy children." But from David to the life of Christ himself, the Holy Scriptures are filled with stories of men and women whose character was such that they could endure night-shift living. Character was such that these dark nights that every human soul has to know could not do permanent wreckage, but could instead be a source of new light and new strength and new power, and new hope.

There are processes at work that will destroy our lives, that is quite true, but there is a kind of character that permits us to turn the nighttime of the soul into the expectancy of new light.

LIFT UP YOUR HEARTS

I REMEMBER ANOTHER DREARY SUNDAY AFTERNOON LIKE THIS. COLD rain dripped from the eaves of a hut in Korea. Hunkered down under the wide eave on his haunches, his crippled fingers twisting at some rice straw mats, there squatted a leper. Never in his life had he had enough to eat; leprosy had horribly disfigured him, but he was singing to himself and to God in the cold and the rain. What does a leper have to sing about?

A day or two later, I met Father Chicetti; short, roly-poly, black-robed, a little string to hold him together in the middle; long white beard, black eyes like deep pools in a very old face. As I walked along at a normal pace he had to trot; his hand reaching up to my shoulder, he looked up at me, smiling. We were walking amidst squalor and the wreckage of half-destroyed buildings. On his shoulders he carried the responsibility for scores of wild-eyed, shaven headed little orphans. They ran in and out, over him and all around him. As he trotted he was humming a song that must have come from his native Silesia, thirty years away. What did he have to sing about?

I remember Miss Susie—I never could say her Korean name. She was an orphan, abandoned, a veteran of the road from Seoul to Osan by way of Yong Dong Po. She spoke a G. I. jargon for English, but hundreds of friends around headquarters understood her and though she wasn't pretty at all, she had a smile like few you will ever see; and she knew dozens of songs and sang them.

I remember Father Rossi. His ideal was the fictional priest, Don Camillo. The story is that Father Rossi had been a prisoner of the Communists for nearly seven years. But he managed to keep himself entertained by rattling the bars of the enclosure until a guard would come by; then he would thank him profusely for keeping the prisoners safe and warm in that nice jail when all the Communists were starving to death on the outside. The guard would curse, and the priest would grin and duck back into the crowd. What did he have to tease about?

I remember a Methodist chaplain. His wife had died a few months before; he was separated by six thousand miles from his children; he had contracted a serious liver disease that now kept him chained to a regimen of spartan control. When I came to his tiny base he moved out of his six- by ten-foot cell in an abandoned textile mill in order that his guest might have the luxuries of a tin stove, a real bed with a sort of mattress on it, and a mirror to shave by. As he carried his belongings off down the corridor I heard him whistling. A stop, and a shuffling of feet as he kicked at a rat, but he didn't even quit whistling. What did he have to whistle about?

You don't have to go too far to hear people who can sing songs in the night. At the University last semester there was a tall and slender hemiphlegic. A blow on the head received in a tank during World War II had left him with a speech difficulty and half of his body unable to function properly; but he has finished a degree in speech therapy. No one knows what it cost him to finish that degree. Now he has opened a clinic to help other people who have speech difficulties.

I remember a tall, freckled, strawberry blonde who had never been away from home until she came here to go to school. Quite by accident she discovered she could sing. Last summer she picked cotton to get the chance to go to choir school.

Over on the East side I have a special personal friend. He is an old preacher, far into the seventies, crippled in every joint. His church is not a big church, but it has a good credit and it has paid its notes, and its people have worked hard to support it. My friend has been preaching now for fifty years. When I went by to see him the other day I suggested that he ought to retire. I wish you could have heard his refusal. He aims to go on just as long as he can move and as long as he can be heard announcing a hymn.

In a tall house on the right side of a certain street lives a man who many years ago had a big post here; for twenty years he has been unable to be away from his bed for an hour at a time. About all he can do is to lie there and teach his parakeet and his neighbors, and be a blessing to everyone who comes by, while his wife does more than any two people I know for children.

On the same street lives a friend of mine who has been to surgery to win half a dozen major battles with cancer. She has won everyone of them—pain, and the awfulness of lying there waiting to learn whether she has won or not. I think she will go on winning them. And back on this side of town I have a friend who from her wheel chair keeps house beautifully for her successful businessman husband who is totally blind. What is their secret?

Whatever the secret it is more than the "power of positive thinking." It is more than a list of mottoes that you repeat when you get in trouble. It is more than the recalling of certain theological and spiritual barbiturates that we can take to keep us from really seeing things as they are. What is their secret?

That rainy Sunday afternoon when I was so impressed by the leper's singing, I was walking down a steep hill with a Korean priest. I had not been able to exchange a single word with him for we had no common language. As we walked, I was regretting that I must leave without having exchanged a single word with him. Suddenly it dawned on me that of course he knew Latin better than I knew English. A phrase from an ancient liturgy popped into my mind, and as I turned away from Father Ha, I said, *"sursum corda!"* A surprised look, then recognition; "Lift up your heart." He answered me, in the bat of an eye, with the congregation's response, *"regem habemas."* "We have a king."

The ability to sing in these nighttimes of life lies in the fact that those who know they have a king understand their nighttimes better. "Lift up your hearts," for, "We have a king," who is not unacquainted with open graves, and griefs, and tensions. He is the hope we have.

BEGGARS IN VELVET

The Life We Lead
The Way We Do
The Hope We Have

CARLYLE MARNEY

Hark, hark, the dogs do bark,
   The beggars are coming to town.
Some in rags,
   Some in tags,
     And some in velvet gowns.

Nursery rhymes may be written for children, but Carlyle Marney points out in the title chapter of this book that their meanings hold a special importance for adults. Basing his discussion on the above familiar rhyme, he offers some unique and wise advice on beggars of all kinds—those who expect to get by on another man's generosity. He especially has some informative things to say about the contemporary beggar in velvet. These beggars, he says, are the great moral threat in our velvet age. Whether doctor, lawyer, preacher, real-estate man, or professor, we will all meet the beggar in velvet. Will we know how to confront him?

The other subjects of discussion here are equally applicable to today's times. Writing in his well-known winsome and down-to-earth style, Dr. Marney offers effective counsel on weaknesses, fears, uncertainties, and desires experienced by everyone—frustration, monotony, aimlessness, confusion, and so on. His witty and humorous illustrations always drive his points home effectively.